KEEPERSOFTHESANDLOT.COM
Coaching, Parenting and Playing for Keeps

By Bill Severns

FOREWORD

The single greatest influence in my life has been my dad. So many of the things that I do now as an adult have traces of him, and his mark on my life will always be on me. Growing up, I took for granted what a great father-figure God blessed me with, but as I grow older and look back on those moments and experiences that shaped who I am, I recognize and appreciate his influence along the way.

Baseball was and still is a big part of my relationship with my dad. As a young player in little league, his encouragement and positive attitude kept me interested in the game and helped me to deal with the ups and downs that young boys go through as they learn to deal with the failures and successes of athletics. Baseball provided an avenue for us to bond while I was growing up; it was something we could easily talk about during those awkward years when a teenage son can be about the most difficult species on earth to communicate with, and it is a love that we both share and appreciate today.

I'll never forget the day before I left for college where I was going to play baseball. My school would be too far for him to see all of my games as he had my whole life up to that point. We went to my high school batting cage so he could throw me one last round of batting practice. I remember thinking how much I was going to miss this lefty who could throw such great strikes. And when we finished, we hugged each other and cried: it was my dad's way of sending me off after eighteen years together.

This book is about baseball, but it is more than that. It is about giving young boys and men the tools they need to grow up and be men and fathers themselves. The coaches of our children should not take lightly the responsibility given to them. Coaching is the opportunity to be a leader, a caretaker, and often a parent to kids who need one. Children can walk around with so many burdens put on them by circumstances at home or peer pressures at school. A coach should provide an atmosphere of growth and development, not fear and intimidation. I think this book addresses what is most important when it comes to coaching young children and it is not protecting the win/loss record, but protecting the hearts and spirits of future coaches, parents, and leaders.

I'm so fortunate to have had such a great teacher in life and coach on the baseball field as I did in my dad. When my own son was born two years ago, I felt ready to be a father and I felt like a man. It was the culmination of years of training and teaching from my best friend and the best coach I've ever had. While fatherhood can be a scary and daunting task, I am confident in the lessons I was taught. And some day when I'm coaching my own children and the children of others, I will remember to pass along the principles and thoughts written down on these pages because I am living proof of the results.

Matthew Severns

• • • • • •

I believe that God has a plan, He has a plan for all of us, he makes us what we are and what we're supposed to be, God made me and Billy Severns baseball coaches. Oh sure, we played the game at the highest levels, and we had some successes, but we were not great players in fact we were not very good at all compared to the everyday major league player. We had a heart for the game, we had passion for the game and most of all we loved playing the game. And through all those experiences God taught us how to be a coach, He put great people in our lives, people who took the time to help develop us as players and people, they cared for us and about us, and because of that we will never forget them.

Baseball is a great game we start playing most of us at a very early age. We learn the value of team work, we learn about work ethic, we learn how to compete, and if we are real lucky we learn that baseball is just a game, meant to be PLAYED. It is not life or death, it is a game. Great coaches realize this and coach that way. They coach to teach, they coach to build up a player not break him down. They coach to develop a young player's life skills for use on and off the field, and most importantly they coach so that their players can make a name for themselves, not so he can make a name for himself. Give all you have for them, all your love, patience, passion, desire, knowledge, positive attitudes, encouragement, compassion, if you ever played this game at a high level you know how hard this game is, from the stands it looks easy but it is not, REMEMBER THAT EVERYDAY!

Billy Severns and I are Baseball coaches at what level doesn't matter because the principles are the same at all levels, little league, high school, college, or pro baseball. Teach your players most of all to have fun, Teach them how to deal with failure as well as success, teach them how to compete, teach them to respect this great game, but most of all teach them how to play the game to the best of your ability (remembering NOBODY knows all there is to know about this game) so just teach them what you know, and do it in a positive loving fun way and they will remember you for the rest of their lives!

Ned Yost - Manager Kansas City Royals
2015 World Series Champions
World's Greatest Turkey Hunter

. . . . . .

In a world that constantly reminds us that winning is the only thing, and losing is not an option we often forget the innocence of sports and the love they were designed to create. Once victory is achieved it is only deflated by reporters asking whether or not the individual or team can repeat the feat the following year. This world demands perfection, yet seems to never be satisfied enough. It seems as if we have lost the wisdom of learning from mistakes. That's what I love about Billy and what he is communicating in the pages to follow. We must return to the days where we allowed athletes to make mistakes and learn from them, not be verbally abused and scarred by them. Every summer I host thousands of teenagers at my camps in the Ozarks and our Philosophy is to never put a kid down, say anything negative, or make them feel as if they have failed anyone. It is the coach's responsibility to encourage, motivate, and inspire the athletes through their shortcomings and make sure they are affirmed and taught through losses and mistakes. I can only pray that more coaches develop the heart Billy has for kids and the purity of athletics. I have been around Coach Severns kids for a little over a decade, and He continually validates everything he says in this book, not by the words he says, but rather the way he continually coaches and loves his boys, both players and family. May we rid ourselves of vicariously living through our sons, win at all cost attitudes, and expectations that exceed what young boys are even capable of and return to the purity, love, and innocence of the game that will only develop lifelong passions within every athlete's heart. I could say that Billy hit a home-run in this book, but that would be a lie! It's a GRAND SLAM!

Joe White
Owner/Director of Kanakuk Ministries
Branson, Missouri

ENCOURAGING POINTERS
(FROM THE PROS) FOR KEEPERS

"Let him play and have fun, or he'll get burned out on the game before he even gets here."

Gene Stephenson
Former Hall of Fame Baseball Coach Wichita State University
Currently the second all-time winningest college baseball coach
7 College World Series, 24 NCAA Tournament appearances,
And Coach of 1989 College World Series Champions

· · · · · ·

"There are two things you need to get right in the early years. Let each child develop their natural abilities and teach them to play fearlessly."

Our influence on children: *"As hard as it is to remember things, we can always remember our great coaches. I'll never forget Coach Maldanaldo."*

Ned Yost
2015 Manager of the Kansas City Royals

· · · · · ·

"Make sure your kids have fun. Tell your parents to relax and enjoy their kid. I can assure you we will find your diamond when he is ready. Putting undue pressure on children to play any sport is a huge mistake."

"Tell your parents we don't have time to scout little league."

Gary LaRocque
Senior Special Assistant to the General
Manager of the St. Louis Cardinals

· · · · · ·

Speaking of violent confrontations, harassment, and bad yelling in general- *"If a kid experiences enough of these violent confrontations in his childhood, he'll quit. We (MLB) will never get a chance to see him."*

"Without Coach Epperson hauling me and my friends all over Oklahoma when I was a kid, I would have never realized any of the dreams I've lived."

"When you yell violently, the exact opposite of what you wanted to happen, will happen."

Stan Meek
Vice President of Scouting for the Miami Marlins

• • • • • •

"Every message you send is received."

Dick Kramer
Former State Championship Baseball Coach
for Shawnee Mission East High School
(Currently Principal of Shawnee Mission North High School)

• • • • • •

"People in Atlanta and around the country ask me how to get their kid noticed at the MLB level. I constantly try and reassure them that MLB simply does not worry about kids in little league. Too much has to happen before they are ready for that pressure."

Joe Simpson
Former Professional Baseball Player with the Los Angeles Dodgers,
Seattle Mariners and Kansas City Royals
Georgia's Sports Broadcaster of the Year, 1995
Current TBS Announcer for the Atlanta Braves (15th Season)

• • • • • •

"We all need these timely and encouraging words. It will help the faithful parents and coaches who are in the trenches fighting the good fight."

John O'Dell
Regional Director – Fellowship of Christian Athletes

· · · · · ·

"I'm a 'keep it simple' guy. This needs to be fun. It's still a little kids game. Let's keep it that way."

"Teach them to think the game, simplify it. . . One pitch at a time."

Brent Kemnitz
Pitching and Assistant Coach Wichita State University – 31 Years
13 Guys to the Big Leagues
68 Pitchers Drafted

· · · · · ·

"The Keepers of the Sandlot is a quick, upbeat and encouraging read for parents, players, coaches and teachers. No doubt our children's actions don't start with a coaches influence or a teachers influence, but with the example set by parents."

Chipper Jones
1999 NL MVP
Two Silver Slugger Award
Founder – Chipper Jones Family Foundation

ACKNOWLEDGEMENTS

All my life when reading a book, I would skip over the acknowledgements as insignificant. Well, anybody who has ever written a book knows that without this page and the sacrificial caring and supportive individuals mentioned, there is no book. There are no words to express what the following people have meant to me in pursuit of this writing challenge.

Without a doubt the biggest sacrifice during the writing process came from the home front. Suzanne, my wife, was always there with her timely insights, incredible patience and her invaluable support. Matthew, Sarah, Drew and Will, my children, contributed each in their own wonderful way. The life lesson here is the value of a supportive family.

Right out of the chute when I expressed this crazy idea of writing a book like this, my dearest friend Gary Colvin says, "Let's do it." Every time I needed encouragement in any form, Gary came through with the way to get it done. I believe that along the way we all benefit from that special person in our life that not only believes in us but takes that special step to motivate and help us.

My mom reminded me that when I was young I always loved to write and gave me that special mother's reassurance that I could do this. We are never too old to listen to our mothers. My dad was always there. He worked long hours and sometimes it was tough, but he got there. When I was cut from my high school team as a sophomore, he was there. He called a friend and got me a spot on a team and a place to play. Because of him and the other dads who showed up to coach us, the MacArthur Bears loved baseball, learned how to play the game, be good sports, and had fun with our friends. I tried to do the same.

Tom Fredrick, my long-time friend took the time to provide me an outline and direction to begin. Without Tom's gift, I wouldn't have known where to start.

Linda Claycomb, my dear friend and administrative assistant for years made one sacrifice after another to keep the manuscript moving along and provide great insight as we moved forward.

Adam Palmer, a brilliant young writer from my hometown of Tulsa grabbed the hundreds of random pages I had written and turned them into the finished product. All along the way I prayed for a "fit" to come along side me and put the manuscript in its final form. Prayer answered.

Again it is impossible to mention everyone but to all of my former parents, players and coaches, thank you. Everyone gave me so much. Thanks for the letters, notes and stories that have gone into this manual. I sincerely hope you enjoyed our time in the Sandlot as much as I did.

To all the contributors from around the country that took my calls and provided countless hours of encouragement, thanks. To my many friends in Kansas City that have so willingly given me encouraging words, especially the gang at the Athletic Club of Overland Park, thank you all.

To top off the whole great ride, Tom and Sherie Bartlett, the owners of DataSource in Kansas City, believed in this book enough to say, "Let's print it." Every day at the Athletic Club, Tom would say the same thing, "When are we going to print?" As I became weary after the 2 year process, it was such a great and encouraging help to see (and hear) Tom's energy and Sherie's support to keep going. Special thanks to DataSource's Production Manager, Charlie Jenkins and Graphic Designer, Chris Untch for bringing everything together, laying it out and working so hard to push this book past the finish line.

Finally, I acknowledge God's hand on this gift He has given me. I prayed many times that if it was His will for this book to happen it would. Half way through the project Drew, my son said to me, "Don't worry Dad, God will meet all your needs." He was dead on and his words are written on my office wall. It turns out, our kids remind us of His hand in all things, what great faith they have.

So to Him who gives us our children, friends and the Sandlot be all the glory.

Bill Severns

TABLE OF CONTENTS

Introduction: Why I Wrote This Book

For as long as I can remember baseball was my greatest passion. If it had anything to do with baseball I wanted all of it. I was just made to play the game and God gave me the desires of my heart. For 22 years I got to play at every level, sandlot, little league, high school, college and professionally. Then when my sons were born I became a coach at every level that 5 to 17 year olds play, from beginners to high school. I coached my own children and all of their friends. I don't honestly know which was more fun, playing or coaching my boys. So for another 22 years I became "coach".

After 44 years of doing something you think you have seen it all. Well, in baseball you see something different every day, every game. I know the game from both sides. From being at the plate with the game on the line, full count and all the pressure on me to hit the game winner to just standing there giving a kid a pep talk before he steps up to the plate in the exact same situation, the game is tough. The great Baltimore Orioles manager, Earl Weaver, once said, "The only thing easy in this game is hustling. The rest is really tough."

However, the toughest role to have and survive the youth sports experience is by far and away that of the parent. Parenting is really tough. As pressures escalate all the way around on all of us it is a wonder we live through it.

So as I searched and wondered what I would be doing to stay in the game as my coaching days came to an end it was revealed to me in a way I never expected.

As I coached third base one night with my 13 year-old Mustangs at bat one of our players hit a hard shot at the third baseman. It took a bad hop and he booted it. This kid happened to be one of my favorite players in the league and reminded me of myself in his love for the game. Well, his coach just let out this thunderous yell that really scared us both! I looked over at him and said, "Hey, come on man, this is a great kid, the ball took a bad hop!" I had never in my 22 years said anything to a coach like that. Well the next time he blocked a ball with his chest and threw it 30 feet over the first baseman's head. He was so tight he

1

couldn't even breathe. The violent confrontation escalated, the coach yanked him out of the game and the rest was just as horrible. I kept looking for his dad, you guessed it, it was his dad.

My heart sank. I felt so bad for both of them, not only for the kid who was being berated for making a mistake, but also for the father who obviously had something going on under the surface that was coming out in his son's direction.

And that's when something clicked inside me, and I knew I had to write this book. I have been given too much and can help parents and coaches relax and enjoy their kids before it is too late. We have to play the game right.

Fortunately, this story has a great ending. The boy actually came and played for me the next year in a tournament. His dad became incredibly remorseful and made everything right with his son. It was great. Hey we parents are humans and kids are unbelievably forgiving!!

Kevin Seitzer, my good friend and current batting coach for the Atlanta Braves, said at breakfast one day, "There are too many kids getting yelled at for making mistakes and committing errors. How are you going to get better at anything if you don't make mistakes? Especially when you are playing baseball - a really tough game to play perfectly. Ask any All-Star in the majors-guys making millions of dollars and they still make mistakes on the baseball field. During the World Series, even."

And they aren't eight years old.

Kids in the modern game are being harassed and yelled at by both coaches and parents and it's taking a toll. It's no wonder the number of kids taking up the game is dwindling. Parents and coaches lament that kids are giving up on baseball. Kids don't give up on baseball; they give up the harassment that we've made baseball.

My ex-teammate and good friend Stan Meek is the Vice President of Scouting for the Miami Marlins. He said this, "If a kid experiences enough of these violent confrontations in his childhood he'll quit. We (MLB, Major League Baseball) will never see him."

If this book saves one kid from this injustice, it was worth it. I had to write this book on behalf of the kids who have to absorb the accelerating pressures of playing a game and who are continually berated for making errors. One of my little league mothers, who got wind that I was writing this book, told me to "write it to the coaches who make kids quit baseball." Her son who was a good player just walked away from the game at age 11. Ouch.

I had to write this book to encourage parents and coaches to enjoy their kids and protect their childhood.

Your children are only children for a few years-they have plenty of time later in life to be adults; it's up to us to guard their childhood, to make it fun, and to protect that feeling of playing in the sandlot.

We're the Keepers of that feeling. We're the Keepers of the Sandlot.

· · · · · ·

I played the game of baseball at every level and loved every day of it, but my days as a player came to an end with torn ligaments. I was in my sixth year of pro ball, playing on the Vancouver Canadians AAA team associated with the Milwaukee Brewers and having a great year. I was hitting .329 at the end of August, looking good, working my way up. But my cleats got hung up on second base during a game and ripped my ankle in a big way.

I received a call from the Brewers brass the next day telling me my time had finally arrived—I was going up to the show for the month of September. There was only one condition: I had to be able to run. I tried for three days to get some speed on that ankle, but it never happened. They put me in a cast for twelve weeks, and my season was over. (Injuries are a great reason to use your college athletic scholarship to get an education.)

In one way, it turned out to be a great blessing in disguise. Being hobbled, being unable to play—it blew out the flame for me and, although I went to spring training with the San Francisco Giants the next year, I had lost the desire to prepare and play the game the way I had done in the past. I walked away from my

3

playing career and never looked back, always thankful that I got to play as long as I did.

More importantly, I had fulfillment. I had lived out my dream, and got it out of my system. I have thought many times that this was huge for my kids, because I never had to live vicariously through any of my four wonderful children. I had my time; I got it out of my system. That was a great help later on when I would occasionally see parents who hadn't gotten it out of their system and were driving their kids to do it for them. That only makes it rough for everyone.

After my career as a player was over, I decided to use my experience to coach the teams that my own children were on. I coached my three sons' teams, guiding them and their friends through their little league years. The first set of kids, the first team, I took all the way through high school. The other two sets went with me through eighth grade.

Our sandlot all these years is a big program in Johnson County, Kansas, called 3&2. Nearly 575 teams compete in these fields every year. It is a big sandlot. The directors, coaches, parents and umpires work diligently year after year to make it great. If you played baseball in Kansas City, 3&2 touched your life.

Jeff Chalk, Executive Director of 3&2, sent me an e-mail with the following statement, which I feel stated clearly how important coaching is. "Since 1951, there have been more than 60,000 players who have played on more than 5,000 teams at Johnson County 3&2; literally tens of thousands. There have been several who have had some level of success going on to play at the collegiate or minor league level, but none have ever reached the major leagues. However, our community is full of former 3&2 league players who have achieved significant success in many other fields of endeavor, including, if not most importantly, coaches of their own sons."

I became a coach to protect my boys—I'd heard too many stories about bad coaches and out-of-control parents.

It really wasn't that bad.

I can't say this enough. Most of the coaches and parents I have come in contact with over my 22 years of coaching have been great. Most coaches have a great heart and coach for the right reasons. They love the game and they love their kids.

4

Sure there are some who have fear
have worry problems, some that have ego
have problems none of us know about. V
some of us just handle them better than oth

And there are a lot of us who have
and enjoying the ride. But the ride is too sl
years, I can say: this ride goes *fast*.

Honestly, I really didn't even understand this un......
eight years, especially the last two as the reality sank in: this was
it. Soon Will, my youngest son, would be in the ninth grade, and
my coaching days would be over. It was maybe the worst feeling
I have ever had.

I finally had a complete view of the big picture. And it only
took 22 years to get there.

· · · · · ·

My dear friend Ned Yost has had a successful career as a
manager in the majors, and I asked him what he thought I should
talk about in this book. His thoughts: "Ultimately, it doesn't matter
at which level we coach, because the principles are the same at all
levels."

1. Teach your players to have fun.
2. Teach them how to deal with failure as well as
   success.
3. Teach them how to compete.
4. Teach them to respect this great game.
5. Teach them to play fearlessly.
6. "But most of all, Keepers, teach them how to play the
   game to the best of *your* ability (remember: nobody
   knows all there is to know about this game). Just teach
   them what *you* know, do it in a positive, loving, fun
   way, and they will remember you for the rest of their
   lives."

I'm going to level with you: the odds of your kid playing
in the big leagues are long, long, long. We'll go into this later, but

ore hopeful players than there are available slots in And yet every MLB team has a pile of scouts looking s who can give them the winning edge, and trust me: if he out there has the ability to play on a major league baseball , they will find him. You don't have to do a thing.

But the odds are significantly higher that your child can learn how to play the game with his friends, learn the basics pretty well, and grow up to be an adult that contribute in a great way to society.

But they'll only get there if their coaches and parents approach the game with a Keeper mentality.

• • • • • •

One of my favorite success stories is a kid I coached named Mike Hughes. Mike loved baseball more than life itself, and gave more effort than most of the kids I ever coached. This kid just never quit, and though he didn't get many hits, he always gave me his best.

This past spring, Mike graduated with honors from the Harvard School of Medicine after doing his undergraduate work at Stanford. His mom said to me, "Bill, you taught Mike to play hard and never to give up, and I think that really helped him with the long hard years of medical school."

When he was on my team, I knew Mike probably wouldn't play in the big leagues, and would never get to "the Show," as we called it. But I also knew that Mike had a big-league attitude, and I knew that if his parents, teachers, and I approached him with a "Keeper" mentality, he would take that attitude on to school and great success. Who knows—Mike may discover a cure that saves my life one of these days.

This is not easy stuff—just *being* a ***parent*** can bring out the best and worst in all of us, and we all have our ugly moments. It's easy to sit in the stands and say, "I just don't understand why all of these parents and coaches are so crazy!" And then things get nuts at home and we suddenly understand how that same feeling can show up on the baseball field. We get crazy sometimes, because we are afraid. We want our kids to be successful and happy.

The fact is we are human. Fortunately for us, our kids love us humans, and are very forgiving when we get a little stupid (especially if we apologize every now and then). I talk to a lot of dads who are carrying some significant baggage, have control issues, worry too much about what the future holds, and are sometimes just kind of grumpy.

But if we can drop the baggage, let the kids have some control back, quit worrying, and be nice, we'd *all* enjoy the game more.

Remember when you were a kid and played the game in the proverbial sandlot? When you used whatever you could find for bases and sometimes substituted a tennis ball and a broomstick because they were available? You just played the game because you were having fun with your friends, not because you were working on your fundamentals or working on your curve ball.

As a Keeper, I had the awesome opportunity to *re-enter* that Sandlot period, to experience baseball as a kid again. To play with my sons and their friends. What a privilege.

· · · · · ·

I played college ball at the University of Oklahoma for Coach Enos Semore, a member of College Coaches Hall of Fame. I asked him what wisdom I should pass on in this book, and he said, "Billy, if you can get these parents and coaches to understand the huge responsibility they have and the *impact* they have on a young man (good or bad) with everything they say or do, you will have done a great thing."

Let's take a look at that:

"<u>Good</u> or <u>bad</u>."

"Everything you <u>say</u> or <u>do</u>."

Kids are watching, whether we want them to or not. They're learning, whether we think we're teaching them or not. They are being molded into the adults they will become, whether we're intentional or not.

Being a Keeper isn't easy; none of this is easy.

Heck, baseball isn't easy. It's a game that's built on failure, honestly. Hitting a baseball is the hardest thing to do in all of sports—it's been documented!

Just for fun, we can go to USA Today's great series on the Hardest Thing To Do In Sports, written by Gary Mihoces and published March 2, 2003. Hitting a 90+ mile per hour fast ball is the hardest. "In his book, The Physics of Baseball, retired Yale University Physician Robert Adair writes that the moment of contact when a bat strikes a ball lasts just 1/1,000 of a second." Obviously, this skill takes years to develop.

Players like Ted Williams and Barry Bonds are absolutely extraordinary athletes and can do things that other people can't. "What is remarkable about them is not their muscles or anything like that. It's their brain," Mihoces states.

"Consider that a fast ball thrown at 95-100 mph reaches home plate in about 0.4 seconds." Adair notes that "it takes 0.15 seconds for humans to voluntarily blink their eyes in response to visual signals. When a big-league fastball is on the way, you must do far more than blink. You must swing the bat to precisely the right spot at precisely the right time." Then there are curve balls.

The sandlot is where we hold up the ball and start the journey. Once you blink, your kid is grown.

Simply put, a player in the majors that hits .300 is considered a master at the plate, but even that level of success means that he is failing *70%* of the time.

So on top of teaching kids this very difficult game, you also have to protect the friendships within the team, keep the parents in the loop *and* manage your parents, all the while guarding the feelings of the whole community. It's a huge responsibility and task. It can be done. It's big picture coaching.

But the most important thing is to make sure the game stays *fun* and the kids learn to play the game. I turn once again to my dear friend and ex-teammate (and major-league manager), Ned Yost:

"Billy, player development doesn't start at my level. It starts at five or six years of age, where you teach a kid to develop his natural abilities and to play fearlessly. If you yell at him all the time, he will draw back and never reach his potential. Tell your parents to not blow it by yelling.

"You get this short period of time to burn your memory into their brains. They will carry these lessons and memories you gave them for the rest of their lives. Don't mess it up."

Think about your goals for your children. What do you want them to live with? What do you want their memories of childhood baseball games to be like? Do you want them to remember your red face yelling at them for being human? Or do you want them to remember having fun with their friends, realizing only in hindsight the lessons they were learning along the way?

Do you want them to remember organized disaster or Sandlot joy?

Let's figure it out together.

Everybody get loose.

Play some catch.

Relax.

Stretch out.

Take a lap.

Choose up teams – everybody in!

The Sandlot is calling our names.

We are its Keepers.

Play ball.

CHAPTER 1

THE SANDLOT AND ITS KEEPERS

"EVERY KID DREAMS OF BEING A HERO...
EVERY KID NEEDS A HERO."

CHAPTER ONE: THE SANDLOT AND ITS KEEPERS

The Sandlot is one of those mystical, magical places in childhood, a place where dreams begin and boys learn the art of working together to accomplish a single goal: to *have fun*! I don't know about you, but when I was a kid, the Sandlot was the perfect place to slip away for many hours, sometimes from dawn 'til dusk. I would disappear with a few friends for the day, and before we knew it, the sun was going down.

We spent time together figuring out the game of baseball on our own, by trial and error, playing as long as we could, until the point where we knew if we stretched the time any further, our mom wouldn't allow us to go the next day. Since that would be sheer torture, we all would head home and start the next day right where we left off.

The summers seemed like endless fun back then, and when we "disappeared" for the day, it meant something so much more innocent than it does now. Today the word "disappear" means an Amber Alert; times have certainly changed.

That's the feeling that we Keepers need to bring back. The safety net of "disappearing," if only for an hour-long practice, is still an important thing to our kids today. But we need to bring that Sandlot feeling back to the game, that safety net. It's up to us, Keepers, to make sure our kids participate in an environment where they can grow, learn, play, and just have fun with their friends. Keepers of the Sandlot are the types of coaches that encourage, protect, teach, engage, and build character into their players; players who will someday become the men and women who lead the following generations.

Keepers must always keep the end goal in mind. Time moves so quickly, and your players are in your care for so little of it. You must use that time wisely and in the best interests of your players. Whether you like it or not, you are a role model, and the way you react to situations will affect the way *they* react.

Being a Keeper is a heavy load.

But it is totally worth it.

• • • • • •

The closest thing I ever got to the Sandlot at the "next" level came during my senior year in college at the University of Oklahoma. We were involved in the dogfight of our college baseball careers as we battled to get back to the College World Series for the fourth year in a row. The previous three years, we'd come away empty-handed, and this year I wanted to win that national title more than anything in the whole world.

But before we could even get the chance, we had to defeat the University of Tulsa and win our NCAA Midwest Regional in Norman, Oklahoma.

I quote now from *The Oklahoma City Times,* May 27th, 1975:

HEADLINE: "OU Takes Title With 'Sandlot' Win."

"It reminded you of one of those old sandlot tournaments Monday as Oklahoma and Tulsa battled their way to game No. 7 of the NCAA Midwest Regional in Haskell Park. OU had downed the Hurricane, 2-1 in Monday's first game to even the tournament, and the winner of the next game would gain that coveted trip to Omaha and the College World Series"

Seven games, three days, everybody pitches, back-and-forth, fever-pitched, endless baseball.

The Sandlot – All day long baseball … everybody in.

Out of pitching...a game like this gets you pumped up... finally found a stopper; when he's on he can be tough...hasn't had a hit in fourteen at-bats; singled up the middle to drive in the go-ahead run...never pitched a kid the next day after throwing nine innings; taking a chance on hurting his arm...picture-book slide... tagged out...record-setting relief pitching...everybody in ...

The mark of a good bunch...faced the minimum through four...out of obscurity, a hero...all guts...unfamiliar pressurized situation...jeers from the opposing bench...mentally tough...a dogfight...endless baseball...

Just as the movies have depicted..our place...where we learned to play the game...just us...friends...anyone can fill a spot and keep it going...no qualifications; nothing required to play... everyone welcome...

A sacred place in our hearts...no adults...no old men yelling...focused and fair...heat...sweat...where we could be kids...

where each of us hits the walk-off home-run...to win Game 7...
Each of us a hero in our hearts...

Do you have a Sandlot in your past? Take a big, deep breath now and remember that time. Go ahead. I'll wait for you.

Let's reclaim that feeling for our kids.

· · · · · ·

In the Sandlot, we all imagined hitting that game-winning walk-off home run, the one that wins the World Series for our team. In game six of the 1993 World Series, Joe Carter of the Toronto Blue Jays hit the *real* walk-off, championship-winning home run, and it is packed with <u>Sandlot joy</u>. If you have ever seen this fantastic moment in baseball history, it is punctuated by Joe's leaping, ecstatic, joy-packed trip around the bases in what is only the second Series-ending home run in baseball history.

If you're fortunate enough to see a photo or video of this great moment in baseball history, take a look at Joe's face. That expression screams, "Sandlot joy!" Every kid has hit that home run in his dreams a thousand times, and every time their imaginary face looks exactly like that. It is absolutely totally kid.

Joe and I go way back; he's from Oklahoma City and used to watch me play at OU. His baseball coaches at Wichita State University were my coaches and best friends while at OU. The man makes me feel old and young at the same time.

I asked Joe about that home run as I wrote this book. "Joe," I asked, "when did you hit your *first* World Series-ending home run?" Secretly, I hoped he'd say that he hit it in the Sandlot.

Joe laughed, "Well, actually Bill, I hit it in my father's gas station when I was a kid." I just started squealing as he told the story, as he went back in time to his Sandlot. Where was your sandlot? Remember when...

Joe's father had a filling station in Oklahoma City, and Joe worked there often as a young boy. "As soon as the cars would clear out and I had a moment, I would get my rubber bands out, and the game would come down to me," he said. "As the announcer,

14

I would first set the scene, bottom of the ninth, game seven, and who else would you want coming to the plate than Joe Carter?" Joe laughed again and flashed that famous smile as he continued to go back in his head and recount the moment.

"I would pull the rubber band tight as it would go and let her fly, then announce the game: 'Joe swings, there it goes, a mighty fly ball... it could be... it may be...' And then I'd watch where the rubber band landed. If it landed on the roof, it was the game winner, and I got to be the hero. 'The ball goes back... and... It's out of here, *we win it all*!' And I would jump around the service station, touching all the bases in my mind, and just take in the moment where I got to be the hero."

Joe got serious for a minute. "Every kid wants to be a hero. Every kid needs to be a hero."

· · · · · ·

Ultimately, we all leave the Sandlot and head out to face the giants. Hopefully, though, we get the *privilege* of returning to the Sandlot with our own children. I chose the word "privilege" on purpose, because it is just that. It is not a right—it is a gift. We have no right to inject *our* agendas on our children's Sandlot. The Sandlot should be classified with "protected" status.

"I had a great time playing baseball for you."

Chase
Mustangs P/OF

Kids need to be heroes, but so do Keepers. Because heroes protect the Sandlot.

Joe Carter's rubber-band dream became a reality in front of all our eyes in the 1993 World Series, and when he told me that he "got to be the hero" as a kid, it reminded me of all the times I would set up the game in my own backyard so I could be the hero. Or the times in our Sandlot when my friends and I would announce our own games and argue over who got to be the hero.

We all want to be the hero when we are little, and Keepers set it up so everyone gets to be the hero.

Without a doubt, my favorite moment every year I coached was at our end-of-the-year party. We'd gather everyone on the team, the moms would fix a huge dinner, the dads would all sit around, and we'd watch season highlights that our cameraman John Stout had worked hours to put together. It was so much fun, just sitting there, recounting the year that had gone by so quickly.

After the highlights, the evening would wind down, and we'd let each boy tell us what their favorite moment was. "When were *you* the hero?" I would say. "Make it about you."

Without fail every one of these kids would start by telling about a moment that *someone* else had that meant the most to them. They really did not want to talk about themselves. We would do our best to make them feel like heroes, and because they felt that way, they were secure enough to focus on their *teammates'* achievements.

Then I got to reinforce for them that moment, remembering it along with them, and adding some other special moments that I had of them. To a boy, for twenty-two years, they *each* had a moment where *they* came through and helped us win.

Moments like these:

"I will always remember the time I was pitching at Nationals. It was real hot. You came to the mound, wiped my face with a cold towel and gave me a bloody nose. It was bizarre. I finished the game and we won." —Chase

"My favorite memory was against the Mill Valley Indians. We were down 2-0 and John and Will were on base and I hit a triple and knocked them in, and we had the game tied, and I got the team motivated." —Carter

"My most famous story with the Mustangs is when I could only open one of my eyes, and I had to pitch with sunglasses on. Ever since then, you and the other players have called me 'Ol' One Eye.' Thanks for making me tough, and a better player." —David

There is something in each of us that makes us want to be the hero. We want to do good things. If we are allowed to try and fail, without getting harassed into oblivion and supported as we learn, we will be ready to answer the call.

My team philosophy was always this: someday it will come down to you, and you need to be ready. Our team will only be great if *everyone* is ready at all times.

We see this in the real world every day, in men and women who respond to the ever-increasing problems in the world. They are the ones who grew up *ready* to sacrifice and put others ahead of themselves.

Keepers are entrusted with preparing the heroes of the next generation. That means that if you are a parent, or a coach, or a teacher who is in the fight, *you are a hero*.

You are a Keeper.

CHAPTER 2

THE JOY OF LEADING

"WE COACH BECAUSE WE CARE...
WE COACH BECAUSE WE WERE COACHED."

Let's talk about why we coach.

We coach because we care.

We coach because we were coached.

Everyone can tell you the name of a coach or two that were exceptional, that contributed deeply to their love of the game and success.

We love being called "coach." It's a great honor. It means your life is (hopefully) impacting someone for the better. It means you have the chance to do it right and for the right reason.

In my years toiling in the minor leagues with the Milwaukee Brewers, I had the privilege of playing with one of the fiercest competitors and greatest teammates I had ever had, my good friend Ned Yost.

In 2007, Ned was the manager of a very young Milwaukee Brewers team, and his players did what very few thought was possible. Not only did they lead the NL Central for the better part of the season, but by the end of the campaign, after they'd been overtaken by the Chicago Cubs they were still in the running to nab the playoff Wild Card spot until the last weekend.

It was an amazing run for a club that everyone had written off in the preseason, but there they were, in the last week of the season, in the thick of it. And in that last week, Ned was thrown out of three games. Ned will fight you to the death, and his team fought for him until the very end.

Ned was asked about his team getting into the postseason after their season ended, and he answered, "Our kids gave their very, very best effort to see that happen. They just fell a little short." [From ESPN – Padres vs. Brewers – Recap – September 28, 2007]

In that answer, Ned personified a Keeper, because Keepers are defenders and protectors. They take the heat for their players. And they keep their players fighting until the last out.

Here's what Ned had to say about it.

"You know Billy, it all starts at the Little League level. It doesn't start in the big leagues. Coaches need to understand that for this short period of time, they get the opportunity to burn their memory and teaching into the hearts and heads of their little leaguers. These kids are at the development phase of their game as early as 5 or 6 years old."

On a business trip to Arizona a few years ago, when Ned was the third base coach for the Atlanta Braves, I asked him to go to breakfast with some business associates of mine. No one even touched their food—they all just listened to Ned talk about the coaching philosophy the Braves used with their players and how they become so successful. And it all boiled down to this one phrase:

"We just want our players to play fearlessly."

He continued: "You cannot be the best if you are afraid. And if you get yelled at every time you make an error, you will become afraid and you will not be able to play the game the way you could have."

Ned hates yelling.

Kids hate yelling.

Everyone hates the yelling.

Quit yelling.

If Ned was speaking to your little league coaching clinic today, he would say this:

1. At this early age, let their natural abilities develop. It will take time. Be patient. Patience is absolutely necessary to be a great coach.

2. Don't miss the opportunity and responsibility you have to influence these kids positively about the game and themselves.

3. Teach them and allow them to make mistakes. Mistakes happen.

4. Teach the boys how to keep fighting even when they get knocked down. This is an essential life lesson to learn.

As parents and coaches, we tend to possibly get a little off-base in our expectations. Instead of trying to drill fundamentals and playing mistake-free baseball into our children's minds, we need to regain a Keeper focus to teach them determination and the joys that come from working hard and accepting responsibility. It's plenty okay to make a mistake as long as you accept it and move on. Just teach them to give all they can and nothing less… and nothing more.

Ned was a third-base coach for the Braves, and I strongly recommend that every Keeper coaches third, at least for a little while. You'll see things in the game you'll never see otherwise.

The actions of a third-base coach live forever in a little kid's mind, so be aware. Never turn your back on a kid when he strikes out; the first place he will look is at you. Be there for him with a smile and the words, "You'll get 'em next time."

Turning your back on a kid is one of the worst things you can do, because actions speak louder than words.

It's up to us as Keepers to keep the game fun. And if you think that's something that's only for Little League, listen to these final quotes from Ned:

"My kids [he calls his team of adults 'kids'!] have a blast. They truly love each other, they *enjoy* each other, they share the passion for the game together, and we love to play together.

"Billy, make sure your coaches understand this: if you compete, whether it is in little league, high school, college, pros, the World Series or whatever, the feelings are exactly the same— no more, no less. They are just as strong for one as they are for the other. As long as we are doing it together, it doesn't matter what we are doing. Enjoy the day right where you are."

• • • • • •

An Epiphany Moment

My third team, the Mustangs, was invited/challenged to travel from Kansas across the state line into Missouri to scrimmage another team. Now, this is the real Sandlot. Our neighborhood against your neighborhood.

We were definitely out of our neighborhood, out of our comfort zone. It was hot. The field was hot and rough. We didn't really know these guys. We just knew they had this look about them that they had gotten us to come to their house and it was time for a different kind of Sandlot game.

(Maybe I'm exaggerating a little. But it sure felt like a showdown-type of atmosphere.)

After the usual pleasantries, the boys were kind of sluggish. They were hot and thirsty and really starting to forget about the game we were about to play and starting to think about lunch instead. We could tell it was going to be anything but our usual Saturday morning Sandlot time.

I wasn't ready for it, and neither was Brad, my assistant coach. Brad designs stadiums and arenas and big sports stuff like that, and he was coming off a busy week of traveling for work. We both just had that look in our eyes.

Why had we come all this way to practice baseball? Why had we left our perfectly good field right by our homes and come all the way over here?

"You want to go get some coffee?" I asked.

"You got that right," Brad quickly responded.

I looked over at the Mustangs and hollered, "Hey, guys, do you think you can manage yourselves while we go get some coffee?" To a bunch of sixth graders. Their response? "No problem, coach. Stay gone as long as you want!"

So Brad and I looked at the opposing coaches and said, "Hey guys, our team can handle themselves. We're going for coffee; we'll be back in a little while."

They looked at us like we were nuts. "What?" they said. What they didn't say, but what we understood, was this: "How can your kids manage themselves in a sixth-grade baseball game? What do you think this is, the Sandlot?"

We talked for a bit, and I finally said to Brad, "You know, I never had a bunch of old men yelling at me when I played in the Sandlot. Did you?" He shook his head. We stood for a moment, just kind of looking at each other, then nonverbally agreed to start our intense search for java.

It took us nearly an hour. But when we got back and saw the kids on the field, we had our epiphany.

It looked like the Sandlot *we* remembered.

They were hustling.

They were yelling.

They were encouraging each other.

They were *coaching*.

They were unbelievably focused.

They were dead serious.

They were chewing each other out. "Hit the cut-off man!" "Run hard all the way through the base!" "Get a good hop!" "Swing! Be aggressive!"

They played any position they felt like, and they did it remarkably well.

They hit.

They fielded.

They ran.

...and they were having a *blast*.

They looked great. We could have watched all day, because the Sandlot used to last all day.

The Mustangs had a great day. And they didn't even get thirsty.

Brad and I joined a couple of mothers under a tree and watched our boys play.

We saw leadership.

We saw teamwork.

Cooperation.

Fire.

Ownership, possession, intensity.

We saw *fun*.

We saw something worthwhile. We watched the Mustangs come together and become the team that would be together for the next three years, the greatest ride of their young lives.

And we learned that our kids did not need *us* to play the game of baseball.

At the end of the game, we had no idea (and didn't really care) who had won, but we knew this team had come together in a way they'd never experienced before.

And they were hungry. Still had lunch on their minds.

As we searched for food, the chatter was unlike anything we'd heard before. Their sweat seemed sweeter. The dirt felt like it belonged. The smiles were huge. The memory will last forever.

And they ate a ton.

I changed the way I viewed myself. I became a different kind of a coach. I sat back more and trusted them to get it done. I relaxed and enjoyed the ride. Likewise, the Mustangs started to view themselves differently. They liked the control they had. They took it seriously. They loved being in charge of their destiny. It was easier on all of us.

· · · · · ·

We are never too old to learn something. I'd been coaching for nineteen years by then, and after all that time, finally I learned the best way to do it: let my boys take possession of their own team. Listen to them. Involve them in the decisions.

It led to the most unbelievable three years I had ever experienced in little league. My boys helped make out the line-ups on the way to the park, got themselves ready to play, assumed responsibility for their own actions, and took care of their own business.

And as a result, they won a whole lot more games than they lost, they took on the giants, and they grew up.

I kind of wish they hadn't grown up so fast.....

CHAPTER 3

A FIELD TRIP TO 'THE K'

"IN MANY WAYS MY RELATIONSHIP WITH MY DAD IS BUILT AROUND BASEBALL — SITTING NEXT TO HIM AT 'KAUFFMAN STADIUM' WITH 2 HOT DOGS LOADED WITH MUSTARD IS HOME."

DAN T.
8TH GRADE LANCERS
UNIVERSITY OF VANDERBILT
MEDICAL SCHOOL, 2010

Chapter Three: A Field Trip to 'The K'

In 1999, I took advantage of a unique moment to reconnect with a dear friend and former coach, Matt Galante. Matt was my manager when I played for the Holyoke Millers, a Double-A baseball affiliate of the Milwaukee Brewers, and he was a great coach.

Being from Staten Island and having had a great coaching career, Matt could tell stories as well as anyone I know. All baseball coaches tell great stories—it just comes with the package—but some are better than others and Matt had some great material. For starters, he was the final pick of the 1966 draft, selected by New York Yankees (What a rush; yours truly was also drafted by the New York Yankees as a junior in college, and I cannot tell you how it feels that the *Yankees* actually pick you. Who cares *when* you got picked?). I bet Matt never topped 5'10", but he had a huge heart for the game and never let any physical limitations get in the way. He always taught that if you were smart, positioned yourself well, and thought things through, you could win.

During the '99 season, the Astros' manager, Larry Dierker had brain surgery, and Matt took over as manager for about a month. During that time, it just so happened that the Astros came up to Kansas City, where I live to play the Royals.

I called Matt when the team got into town and he immediately invited me and my sons to come to "The K," Kauffman Stadium, on Sunday morning, meet the players and tour the clubhouse.

We were there in a matter of minutes and what a great day we had. Matt was as gracious as ever and my sons got to meet the players, while I was able to see some old friends who were now coaching for the Astros. It was truly sweet.

(If you have never had the treat of seeing a big-league clubhouse, try to find out a way to do it. Food everywhere, candy, seeds, music, a hot tub, rub-downs, hundreds of everything, gloves, bats, balls, loud laughter... camaraderie at its finest. It is a place unlike any other; the ultimate dream come true for anyone.)

As game time approached and the routine of the players and coaches started to focus, we could tell that it was time to leave. Game time in the big leagues is very intense. Go a few days without a hit, blow a save, or make an error, and you can be gone.

But for me the best was yet to come.

As we drove out of the parking lot, my oldest son Matthew, who was 19 at the time said, "Gosh, Dad, that really is the life isn't it?"

I remember this as clear as day. "Yeah, buddy," I said, "it sure is. But you know what I would really hate about it?"

"What?"

"Matt never got to coach his sons."

I don't even remember Matt's sons very well. I know there was a Matt, Jr. because Matt, Sr. talked about him quite a bit. I know he was very proud of him.

I continued. "I don't think I could have taken it to not be able to coach you boys."

A silence came over the car. Matthew and Drew were thinking.

· · · · · ·

There is a price to pay for success in the big leagues. Everything has a price, of course, but this price is a steep one. First of all, there isn't much job security when it comes to coaching at the professional or even college level. Matt was with the Astros for 21 years, and in that time, there were five managers, six general managers, and two owners. Matt coached first base, third base, was a bench coach, and then he was gone. Not exactly a stable lifestyle.

Most people only see the fun stuff. Matt was credited with teaching Craig Biggio how to play second and worked with Jeff Bagwell and Ken Caminiti to help them be successful.

But in all that time, Matt never sold his home in Staten Island. While he was born to coach, he never really knew where he would be coaching from year to year.

And on top of that, being a coach in the big leagues means traveling all the time. You're away from your family nearly all year long. You miss seeing your kids grow up. You miss almost everything. Instead, you're working with "other" kids, known as "professional ball players."

I have always been thankful that I got to coach my "actual" kids.

• • • • • •

We're still making our way out of the parking lot of "The K," and there were those blank stares on my son's faces. I could almost see the wheels turning inside. What? Dad not coach us? That would be inconceivable. Would the price be worth it?

Two weeks later, as we are leaving the 3-And-2 baseball complex where my boys played, Drew then about twelve, said to me, "Dad, I figured it out. I'm going to play pro ball until my first son is five, and then I'm going to quit so I can coach him."

I am always amazed at the minds of kids. It took him two weeks, but Drew had worked through the dilemma. He wanted it all and he figured out a way to make it possible.

Kids need their dads and coaches.

I wouldn't trade coaching my sons for all the money in the world or for a spot in Cooperstown. I know I didn't have all the success that the world craves at the big-league level, but I don't really regret it. Why? Because I have no regrets with my boys. I certainly wasn't perfect all the time, but I was there for most of it. That's what they wanted.

All my boys are, for the most part grown now and now my best investments are walking around, making investments themselves, in their wives, in their children, and in their careers.

Not a day goes by that one or two of my kids doesn't walk through the door on their way to something. One of them will call and check on us, or ask for a little help or encouragement, or, in the case of my youngest, ask when we are eating dinner and if they could stop by. The best is when we get the call asking if they can drop off a grand-kid for a while.

Now there is a return on an investment.

CHAPTER 4

GET OUT OF
THE DUGOUT

THE CIRCLE WILL NEVER BE BROKEN

Chapter Four: Get Out of the Dugout

My team, the Mustangs, had a ritual. It was their idea, and they did it every game. It was the "Circle in Center Field." The boys would go to center field, get in a huddle, and talk. No one knows what they would say during this time, but we all knew it was very important to every one of them. Even my own son never shared it with me, and he shares *everything* with me. But instead of trying to figure out what they were saying, I would always just marvel at how dedicated they were to whatever they were doing there. It was a group of friends coming together in unity over something they will never forget.

I bring that up as an example of getting out of the dugout. We've all heard the phrase "out of the box," but now I want to talk about "getting out of the dugout." Basically, it means that we not only focus on the game and the basics of it, but we also put an emphasis on *enjoying* the game. Even loving the game.

"How you coached us and handled our team made it so much more fun."

John
Mustangs Catcher

Ask your kids what their main goal in being on a baseball team is. Go ahead. I'll predict their answer: they are there to have a great time with their friends. Most of them could care less about which one hits or pitches the best. Of course they want to win, but that isn't their main goal.

Somehow over the years, we adults tend to lose that aspect of our lives, and we turn everything into a competition. We want to *win* at whatever we are doing. In baseball, we want to beat the other team. In business, we want to beat our competitors. At the movies or a sporting event, we want the best seats. How many of us get out of bed saying, "I'm so excited to get up and go to work today!" Sometimes, we lose the magic we once had as kids and get into a rut.

As Keepers, we need to remember that the kids on our team are still in that magic phase of their lives where they *are* excited to get out of bed, especially if they have practice or a game to look forward to. And even then, it often isn't even about the game or the practice; it's about a chance to be with their friends.

I always marvel at the arrival of some teams to little league games. Some coaches are so organized it is amazing. For over 22 years I have watched in astonishment at the precision and purpose of some teams. Likewise, there are teams that you see and wonder if all nine players will show up to even have a game.

Both teams can be dangerous. I have always been so appreciative of the assistant coaches who have filled in the administrative tasks of game-day preparation, and the mothers who have somehow managed to get everyone where they were supposed to be even when the instructions, times, and directions were extremely vague.

When I first started coaching, I was pretty militant about the way my teams showed up at the park, but over the years, I began to be less rigid. Maybe it was because of a coach I served under for a while, a guy who would arrive at practice in full dress, screaming one thing after another at the boys. They looked at him like he was crazy. He would spew instructions and random thoughts around the field, and the boys would glaze over with information overload. I did, too.

It was almost like they wanted to say, "Excuse us coach, but we don't *work* for you. We're just here to play some baseball."

I started to realize that as the boys got older, it was to my advantage and theirs to let them develop their own routine. I let them take control of their team, and as I did so, shepherding them along the way, they really started to do a better job of getting ready. They learned how to roll into a game and it became very fun to watch.

"Whether we dominated or got dominated, you always made it into a learning experience."

Robert
Mustangs P/SS

Most days they got ready.

Some days they didn't.

They learned the difference in coming ready to play.

That was when they started the Circle in Center Field. I don't know which player started it, I don't know what was said, and none of the Mustangs ever volunteered that information to me. Of course, I never asked.

All I knew was that before every game, one of the boys would just kind of initiate a movement that called everyone to the warning track in center field.

Each Mustang headed that way.
It was a quiet time, and we didn't start until it was over.
The Circle will never be broken.

. . . . . .

Ron Berler wrote a wonderful article in *Sports Illustrated for Kids*, summing up a survey they did. In this survey, they asked one thousand boys and girls from grades one to twelve, from all over the country, what they wanted in a coach for their team.

What did they say? All sorts of things:

- Make us better players.
- Play everyone.
- Keep the focus on fun.
- Be a friend.
- Yell, but only the good stuff.
- Believe in our abilities.
- Encourage teamwork.
- Teach us the game.

The usual stuff, wouldn't you say? But did you notice anything missing? Would you like to guess what the kids cared about the least?

"Winning."

Winning came in dead-last.

My favorite line in the article was from a boy in Northfield, Illinois, who said, "I like winning a lot, but if you win and don't have fun, it's like losing." In all my years of playing and coaching I have never heard a line as dead-on as that.

The survey also listed several personality types and asked the kids to choose the type of coach they wanted to play for. Good news, Keepers: the answers were pretty evenly divided. Kids would play for just about any personality type—including *yours*! They are really pretty serious about why they play, and while they mostly want to have fun, they also want to learn and become better ballplayers in the process.

To me, this really emphasized the ability that kids will

adapt to various coaching styles. Nobody has the market on one successful style. But as coaches, you need to understand that, of the fifteen or so players you have on the team according to this survey, about a third of them will easily play for you. The others will have to adapt to you and your style, and though it will take some work, they'll get there.

This is why I think it is much easier to coach in the Sandlot years with as many assistant coaches as you can get. Encourage other dads to be a part as much as possible. The kids love seeing their dads there. And dads, you'll never regret the time you take off your tie and show up for practice. Keepers, trust me: it is much easier to share the load with other great dads. Don't worry about being a professional baseball player or expert on anything, just get out there, mix it up, and make a few great memories while you have the chance.

(Other interesting parts of the survey included this statistic: 60% of the kids did not want their parents to give advice to the coach on how to run the team. I about died when I saw this.)

Maybe the biggest challenge you'll face is finding the right amount of playing time for each kid on your team. From my experience with the Mustangs and the other teams I coached is that they (the kids) were extremely sensitive to their friends' feelings and playing time. It is probably the toughest thing we have to navigate through when the little league teams are full. I have coached with as many as seventeen players on a team, and it is difficult.

As only a kid could say it, this boy from California was quoted in the article: "Everybody should play the same amount so that everybody has the same amount of fun."

I remember a game one night watching Drew's freshman team play it was so cold I sat in my car with a friend to get out of the weather. The nine kids who *weren't* playing were all huddled together on the bench and seemed to be having as much or more fun than the nine who were in the game. Kids just want to be with their friends.

Look at the game through the lens of a child's eyes and see what they want, desire, and need.

Our lens is different. Look at them like the parent, coach

or teacher you are. Get eye level with them and understand where they are coming from.

Give them both what they want and what you know they need. It isn't easy, but you'll never do anything more worthwhile or rewarding. Your kids will love you for it.

"I've learned lessons that will help me the rest of my life."

Peter
Mustangs 2B

CHAPTER 5

THE CHALLENGES
OF THE KEEPER

DEVELOPING
LEADERS

"GUIDE WITH YOUR HEART,
LEAD WITH YOUR BRAIN"

KEEP
FRIENDS
TOGETHER

COACH DEICHLER

CONQUERING
GIANTS

KEEP
YOUR
SANITY

BETTER
COMPETITION

ENJOY
THE
RIDE

GIVING
COURAGE
TO LEAD

KEEPING THE
NEIGHBORHOOD
TOGETHER

CHAPTER FIVE: THE CHALLENGES OF THE KEEPER

I am asked a lot about competition: Shouldn't my kids play against better competition? What do I do if we need more competition? We've played everyone around here; shouldn't we want some better competition? Usually I'm asked this in order to justify a parent moving their child from one team to another in the name of "competition." Many parents are discontented with simply letting a kid play wherever his or her friends are playing, and while I understand this discontent, I think we need to look at the bigger picture. The competition is coming…trust me.

Yes, there is an advantage that comes from playing "better" competition—it stretches your team and helps them "play up" to the level of their opponent, but my experience tells me that this perceived advantage significantly pales when you separate kids from their friends. My opinion: when you split a kid from his friends to play for a better team in the name of competition, you may be harming your kid more than you're helping them.

Children seldom, if ever, choose to de-select their friends. Parents and coaches do.

Children hate to be singled out. No one likes to be alone, but it's especially true when it comes to kids.

The desire to separate childhood friends in the name of "better competition" is a control issue that really misses the mark and creates a strain. Another thing to consider is unless you move out of town, your child, once he or she reaches the high school level, will have to come back to the pack and mix back in. This creates an unfortunate attitude that says "I'm better than you guys but I have to come back." Even if the kid handles it gracefully, it isn't natural and really puts strain and added pressure on everyone, including the kid. There is a significant chance that the ones who have to accept him back may push him away.

Instead, in the Sandlot years, you need to just enjoy the ride. If your kid is the best player on the team, then just be the best. Let them have fun with their friends. Lead them to championships! Sure, you may have to "drag" a few buddies around, but what's wrong with that? Won't it make you better and more liked if you can do it?

Look, anybody can put an All-Star team together, but even then, you aren't guaranteed to win—it doesn't even always work on the major league level (the Yankees are consistently the highest in payroll, and it's been awhile since they won it all).

Our Mustangs had every level of player on our team, and none of my players ever, and I mean *ever*, classified their friends as lesser than themselves. Instead, it was very refreshing and positive to hear my kids defend each other instead of blame each other, and it's something we adults would do well to learn. Listen to your kids!

"The Mustangs are great friends, have a lot of heart, and a fun team to play for."

Dylan
Mustangs P/SS

This is a big picture attitude.

· · · · · ·

One of the greatest joys of coaching in the Sandlot is seeing the way my kids have enjoyed their teammates. From the minute they hit the park for practice, there is that buzz of friendship, the attempts at playing catch, the inevitable overthrows, the chasing of one errant ball after another (I always joked that the game is called "Catch," not "Launch and Chase"). It was just a time to get together and enjoy the company of friends.

As a Keeper, you have to realize that *this* is the time we used to have in the Sandlot on those great summer mornings. No hassles, no pressure. Who cares if we chase a few? We *will* get better at it if we just get enough time to practice. Unfortunately, in today's Sandlot, that time is harder and harder to find. Everyone is in such a hurry, the fields aren't available forever, and often too many teams are scheduled.

So, to recapture that Sandlot feeling, I had many, many practices where I just let go and watched the kids have fun. This approach drove some of my assistant coaches (and parents!) crazy, but they eventually learned to enjoy it with me.

Baseball is all about the team. It is, in a quirky way, an individual sport in the sense that, at any given second, if the ball heads your way, it is up to *you alone* to make the play. But first and foremost, you are a part of a team.

I have played on great teams. Some had great talent; some had less. Some had hardly any talent, but great chemistry, and I won a lot more on those teams than on ones that oozed talent—and selfishness. This is not something new. I bet nearly every coach can tell a story of a team with less talent that won it all. Matthew's high school coach, Dick Kramer, who won a high school state championship, said to me, "You win state championships with over-achievers."

At the beginning of each of my 22 years coaching at the little league level, I started with a speech that would hopefully make each kid realize his need to prepare and get ready to help us win. It would go like this: "We will only be as good this year as our weakest link. I have no idea who that is. We all have distinct and different capabilities to help us win. One of you may be the best pitcher, one the best hitter, one the best fielder, one the best bunter, one the best runner. Doesn't matter. Sooner or later, it will come down to you. It will all be on the line one day and *you* will have to come through. But I have faith in you to do it."

"You brought out the best in me."
Jack
Mustangs P/RF

If I say anything that has been true over the years, this is it. This single point makes everyone realize they have a job to do, while also helping them realize that there are other kids on the team who have talents they don't.

• • • • • •

Whitney was a fighter. The kid had energy, wiriness, mental toughness, a competitive spirit… and a lack of knowledge in how to use it all. It led to a lot of frustration with baseball, frustration that threatened to drive him crazy. But he never gave in to it. He was always ready to do something to help, and he always did a great job of keeping his emotions in check.

Teams *always* reflect the attitude of their coach—it's up to you, Keeper, to set the pace. And every now and then, you'll get a kid like Whitney. He was a treat to coach.

Whitney's natural talent won several ball games for us over the years but his greatest moment came while I was away. I heard about it when my oldest son Matthew called me, overflowing with excitement about Whitney and how he had won a game for us against our number one rival.

It was the bottom of the seventh, score tied, and Whitney was on third base. Now, over the years, Whitney had often hesitated on the bases, having difficulty balancing his desire to run against his desire *not* to make a key mistake (it takes time to learn how to gauge these things). Well, with all of the excitement and the importance of the game and the score tied, Whitney got the balance right and seized the moment.

The pitcher wound up and bounced a ball that got by the catcher. Whitney took off, and, in Matthew's words, "He flew across home plate headfirst like Superman and we won!"

Being a teammate means being prepared to help in any way you can.

Shortly after that, Whitney discovered wrestling, and the frustration was gone. It was a great sport for his energy, quickness, and mental toughness. I would hate to wrestle Whitney.

He gave up baseball, but he never gave up the lessons he learned while *playing* baseball. We allowed Whitney to make mistakes, and we allowed him to learn how to be a teammate while staying an individual. And when it came down to it, Whitney was in the game for friendship, not for better competition or to get ahead in life.

As Keeper, you are obligated to protect not only the kids, but also their friendships. Time will separate them soon enough—you don't need to separate them artificially in the name of "competition." There will come a time for that soon enough.

Sandlot Coaches should adopt this motto. "Keep friends together." Let them play at a level where they can *all* be successful, and gradually turn up the heat by finding tougher leagues for them to compete in. Hardware is good. Win some trophies at the lower level, if that is what it takes to grow the team and their confidence.

But don't stay there. Move them all up *together* and they'll all learn how to compete.

Hardware is good for kids. Winning is great, especially when they get to walk the halls at school for a little while as champions. And, by the same token, when they *lose*, they *still* get to walk the halls together, all the while learning that it is good to have teammates in the same boat when they lose. Baseball, after all, is full of losing.

The point is that kids need to do these things together. Which means it's up to you to accept the challenge of making *all* of them better players instead of going out and trying to find great players by separating friends at such an early age.

> "*I know my friends will always remember how you made us a great baseball team.*"
>
> Will
> Mustangs P/ 3B

Really all that matters is that your team thinks they are a great team. They'll be happy.

The Mustangs were not the best team in the world by any means. But we were a fun team, and we made memories. Memories that those kids will *share* for the rest of their lives. It's hard to share a memory with a stranger.

• • • • • •

In my journey through elementary, high school, college, and pro baseball, there were a couple of words that I think need to really be understood by parents of young athletes and coaches. Those words are "potential" and "compare."

First, **potential**. This is a huge burden for any kid to bear. It is really easy for people to lavish great praise on a kid and to let everyone know what their expectations are for that kid. The problem is that *the kid* then has to live up to it. And if he doesn't, he's considered a failure. Going back to Ned Yost's advice, how is the kid going to play fearlessly if he's constantly worried about not living up to his "potential?"

Is that really what you want? The curse of "potential" is not fair for children to have to deal with—certainly not when they are in the Sandlot years. They have to taste every sport and challenge that comes their way, and that takes time. Each sport teaches a different skill-set. Some kids are built and meant to play certain sports and certain positions, and that's a tough thing to figure out.

My kids have often wondered why I set a batting line-up the way I do. It starts with classifying the boys in two groups: "Gazelles" and "Pachyderms." Fast and not-quite-so-fast. When it comes to baseball, it isn't good to get the gazelles stuck on the base paths between pachyderms; it's better for the pachyderms to drive in the gazelles.

This always wound up being a fun thing that led to many speed contests. Pachyderms tend to take it personally, and they usually worked hard to improve their speed. Meanwhile, the gazelles just loved to run so a pachyderm can't catch them. I'd set up races, and when a pachyderm finally caught a gazelle, there was a lot of rejoicing.

Second comes **compare**. Another burden to bear. Comparing one kid to another is just asking for trouble. Kids are all different, they're all unique, and they all bring something to the table. Someone is always going to be bigger, faster, and stronger; someone else is always going to be smaller, slower, and weaker. But the result of comparing the two kids is *either* a general feeling of superiority that sets your team up for defeat *or* a resolution in your players' minds that you cannot win, which, again sets you up for defeat. At its worst, comparison can bring you *both*.

The fact of the matter is, your kids are going to compare themselves to other players on the team. That's just human nature, and there's no way around it. When I was pitching in the fifth and sixth grades, I compared myself to Randy Wilson, the best, most feared pitcher in our school. No way did I match up, but no way did I ever admit that. And though I compared myself to him for a bit, I never got obsessed with it. If I had, I would never have kept going.

But don't let the comparison game come into *your* part of the team. Yes, you have to recognize the strengths and weakness of your individual players, you have to sort out the gazelles and the pachyderms, but don't waste your team's time and energy by trying to point out who is the best player on the field. Let the kids be themselves, and, ultimately, they'll reward you for it.

As I gathered information for this book, I had a wonderful conversation with a young man who played all the way from little league to college. As he talked about his high school teammates, he said, "There were some who were better than me, but they just kept quitting and I kept playing."

Keep playing, and you never know what might happen

I've seen a lot of kids disappear in my 22 years, and they disappear for all kinds of reasons. Different interests, different skills, different friends, stress, burnout, emphasis on another sport... the list goes on.

Here is where the Sandlot philosophy has to help. Parents and Keepers, have the courage to stand back and let the system weed out the competition. There is an incredible amount of fallout in a system where kids are put under so much pressure at an early age. And when I say "early age," I mean all the way to age 15 or 16. The mistake of applying all of the competitive pressures on every single thing in a kid's life in an effort to "make them the best" or to "give them every opportunity" will cause them to lash out at all of it and give up.

Consider Elena Delle Donne, a highly recruited basketball player in high school who accepted a scholarship with the University of Connecticut, one of the perennial powerhouses in NCAA Women's Basketball. After two days of classes in her freshman year at school, she left college, burned out on basketball.

Elena later enrolled at the University of Delaware and walked on to the volleyball team, a sport she'd never played before. And suddenly, she was happier. She enjoyed sports once more.

Her volleyball coach, Bonnie Kenny, summed it up like this: "No kid should have to go through what she went through... Adults need to pay attention. These kids are burned out From 12 to 18, I bet Elena could count on her hands the amount of weekends she didn't have anything to do related to sport. She's missed the opportunity to be a kid." [ENDNOTE: *The New York Times,* "At Pinnacle, Stepping Away From Basketball," by Jere Longman, October 18, 2008, accessed at http://www.nytimes.com/2008/10/19/sports/ncaabasketball/19athlete.html?_r=2&oref=slogin&oref=slogin]

Don't make them miss the opportunity to be *kids*. They'll have plenty of time to be adults later in life, when they're adults.

Our Sandlot philosophy of being a great neighborhood team is that we are all going to be around a long time together, so it will ultimately benefit all of us if we enjoy the ride together. It can be great for a lifetime.

"I loved stealing second, third and home. Best of all our team was a great place to be with our friends in a great environment and no one cared if you screwed up as long as you tried your hardest."

C.C.
Dragons CC/Pit/IB/OF

"Coach, I loved it because you had such a passion for the game and I could tell you enjoyed it as much as I did. Thank you so much for letting me be a part of something so memorable."

Nick
Dragons 3B/Pit

"I learned a lot about life playing baseball."

George
Dragons OF/CAT

CHAPTER 6

THE ODDS

"THE SURE BET IS TO MAKE THE SANDLOT YEARS A GREAT LIFE-LONG EXPERIENCE FOR PARENTS AND KIDS, FAMILIES AND TEAMMATES AND THEIR COMMUNITY. I DON'T KNOW HOW TO SAY IT ANY SIMPLER THAN THAT"

GARY LAROCQUE
ST. LOUIS CARDINALS

Chapter Six: The Odds

Trying to predict the future has always caused me a lot of grief. I think as parents we worry too much. The inward struggle to help our kids "beat the odds" occasionally causes us to get crazy. Have some faith. Let faith replace worry. If you let them your kids will take you on a great trip. There are lots of "fields" for them to potentially play in.

So, what exactly are the "odds of a kid making it all the way to the big leagues?

Well, they are long to say the least. But the question can be answered in a fun way. Since we are talking about the years of the Sandlot, (around 5 to 16) it is really impossible to place a serious or meaningful number here. There are just too many things that have to happen over these 10 years. This is an exploratory time for a kid as well as parents to determine which sport or profession they will have the most passion for. All of the experts will tell us that and this is a great reason for parents to relax and let these interests develop.

However, the NCAA does have a great web-site that answers the "odds" question once they become high school seniors and is worth a look at www.ncaa.org. The statistics are fascinating and give us a look at what the odds are in many sports or as we would say the "sandlots of choice". I think these numbers are very reasonable, look it up and see for yourself.

For the sake of this book, we can briefly look at the baseball example. The web-site states that since these numbers show the chance of getting drafted by a major league team, not of playing, the true odds are even lower.

For high school seniors who will go on to play NCAA men's baseball, the odds are 3 in 50 or 5.6%. To me, this is encouraging and about what I would expect. If a kid has the ability, loves the game and still hungers to play, a college dream is certainly attainable.

Next, for NCAA seniors drafted by a Major League Baseball (MLB) team, the odds are 11 in 100 or about 10.5%. If you can get a college degree and still get to play college baseball, you will have been very blessed.

Finally, the web-site states that a high school senior signed by a MLB team will have a 1 in a 200, or 0.5%. Drafted players almost always go to a minor league team. These teams abound; there are over 150 of them, compared to 30 in the majors. The big leagues have 750 players, yet the 2004 draft alone took 1,500. Hence, some estimate that only 1 in 33 minor leaguers ever makes it to the pros. The web-site concludes that if that's correct, the chance of a high school player making it to the big leagues is 1 in 6,600 or 0.015%. That's roughly the chance of a thief guessing your PIN number on the first try.

My recommendation would be that if your kid gets drafted and signs out of high-school, make sure he gets a ton of money.

I would tell my boys that "one day daddy won't be able to do it for you". I wanted them to go out with confidence, knowledge and a love of the game.

What about the odds of a kid growing up to be a confident young man or woman who has a great love of the game and who contributes in a big-league way to society, raises a great family, and passes on their love of sports to their kids?

Which do you think is more likely to happen?

Don't get me wrong, I would *never* tell a kid he couldn't make it to the big leagues ... ever.

But it's not really up to me, or to you, or even to your kid to force their way into the majors. I've talked to many big-league scouts, and they've all told me the same thing: There is a system in place to discover your kid if he is destined for the big leagues. If he has the talent, *they will find him.* He can stay right where he is, enjoy his friends, and still get to the big leagues. In the meantime, your kid can live his life and decide for himself whether he wants baseball to be a part of his life. Either way, your child wins – this is the best.

Your kid really needs you, but eventually they have to make some decisions for themselves, without you. This is how we learn.

When I signed my very first professional baseball contract (not a very big one), I headed out from the University of Oklahoma and the College World Series to a small town in upstate New

York called Newark (which is not the same city as Newark, New Jersey).

I was a Newark Co-Pilot, and I was lost. Fortunately, Gary LaRocque found me. Gary had been in camp for a couple of weeks and introduced himself to me as my new best friend. Since he'd graduated from the University of Hartford in Connecticut, he at least had a better idea where we were than I did. (I still wondered why we weren't in New Jersey). We had a great couple of years playing together in the New York Penn League, and again two years later in Holyoke, Massachusetts on a double-A team for the Brewers. Gary and I have been the best of friends for over thirty years.

Here are some credentials on my friend Gary: he is currently the Senior Special Assistant to the General Manager of the St. Louis Cardinals. Over his 32-year baseball career, he's had various roles with the New York Mets, Los Angeles Dodgers, and Milwaukee Brewers. He has managed several minor league teams, and served in senior management levels since 1998 as Scouting Director, Assistant to the General Manager and Vice President of Player Development and Scouting.

Can we all agree Gary knows what he's talking about? Here's his advice to you, Keepers (and parents): "Make sure your kids have fun, and tell your parents to relax and enjoy their kid. I can assure you we will find your diamond when he is ready!"

Get that?

Let's continue, as Gary offers help on how to relax and enjoy the Sandlot years:

"The number one thing that baseball should be for a kid is fun. Scouts across the board will tell you that. The biggest part of the adventure when you are twelve years old is to have fun. Putting undue pressure on children to play any sport is a huge mistake."

Gary is a parent. We have often talked about his daughter Ashley. The pressure for her to perform in soccer was so intense, she decided not to play as a freshman in high school. Just gave it up. She didn't want to have anything to do with soccer. She was told she would be an All-State goalie, and she chose not to play.

Then her senior year, she decided to play. She was the goalie. Her team won the State Championship. She had college scholarship potential and she stopped playing. She didn't want to play anymore.

So Gary speaks from a parent's perspective as well as a scout's perspective. I asked him further questions, like:

What do scouts look for?

What system is there to assure parents their kid can make it?

What can parents do to cheer their kids on?

—and—

What are the odds these days of getting to the big leagues?

• • • • • •

Gary was an education/math major in college, and he has shared some great statistics with us. I trust we can all agree in the validity of these numbers, which he based on four years of player drafting, from 2000 to 2003 in the MLB Annual Drafts:

(During that time, approximately 6000 players were drafted, or about 1,500 per year. Thirty teams drafted each year for a maximum 50 rounds. Obviously, not all of the players signed. The numbers reflect how many have made it to the Major League (ML) level. The numbers are constantly changing with each passing day, as players move up and down, therefore, the word 'approximate' is used often. Finally, these numbers are based on what is called major league service time, or days spent at the ML level.)

- **7.6%.** The percentage of players drafted that have played at least *one day* of ML service time. (458 players had service time of at least one day out of the approx 6000 drafted)

- **227.** The number of players drafted between 2000 and 2003 with more than *one year* of ML service time.

- **119.** The number of players drafted between 2000 and 2003 with more than *two years* of ML service time.

- **45.** The number of players drafted between 2000 and

2003 with more than *three years* of ML service time (that's less than 1%).

And that's not including players like, for example, Daisuke Matsuzaka from the Boston Red Sox, who was never drafted, but who came from playing overseas. The big-league marketplace is becoming more and more crowded as the game goes global, and the odds of making it to that level are getting longer and longer. No matter how hard you try, you will never force your way into that market.

Instead, trust Gary and others like him when he emphatically says, "Good players will be seen!" Always on the search for a competitive edge, the pros have several hundred scouts in every nook and cranny of the world looking for the next star. How do you get as much exposure as possible? Just keep playing!

• • • • • •

Well, that's all fine and good, but what should you, as a Keeper, work on with your kids? What are the scouts looking for? And what skills will help your team overall? When a Scout is at a game, among other things he hopes he can see a player's:

- Hitting ability.
- Power potential.
- Running speed.
- Arm strength.
- Fielding ability.
- Effort.
- Desire.
- Makeup.

When a scout is at a game, he may not see, but will eventually want to learn:

- Player's makeup.
- Player's knowledge of playing the game.
- Player's effort.

Gary scouted and signed David Wright of the New York Mets. While it was obvious then, as it is now, David is a true superstar in every way, but what I found fascinating, and is something we can teach our kids early in the sandlot years, is that when Gary went to see David play in high school, he noticed something beyond his physical baseball talents and skills. After a round of batting practice and hitting the ball all over the park and "out" of the park, David took time to go chase the ones over the fence that had gone onto the track. That told Gary about David's sense of responsibility and character. Scouts are looking for great ball players *and* great character in guys. Hustle is the one thing that is easy to do. Everyone can hustle, no matter what level, and people will notice. Good character, on the other hand, is a quality that an individual has to choose to develop. It takes greater discipline to have good character.

Responsibility and character can be taught, developed and understood by young kids and coaches. If David Wright could do it, your kids can, too.

Gary, again: "That really helps... *parents* relax, because it is totally irrelevant for little league at this point. We scouts have too much to worry about at the high school, college, and pro levels to worry about little league. We don't scout little league baseball.

"The sure bet is to make the Sandlot years a great lifelong experience for parents and kids, families and teammates, and their community. I don't know how to say it any simpler than that."

I still wasn't satisfied. So I kept pressing him to answer the question and tell me what it took for a kid in little league to get to the majors.

"Ultimately, we scouts have to project whether or not a player will fall in the 7% of all drafted players that make it for at least one day and have the ability to hit .265 and 17 home runs a year to just be an *average* ballplayer."

Just to be average. Go back to the numbers we just went over and remember that we are talking about very few players that are still left out of 6,000 in a 4 year span.

Gary: "Now this kid has to not only have those exceptional physical capabilities, but the resolve to handle the pressure and makeup to survive a 162 game schedule. It is ridiculously tough. This is what we talk about when we say makeup, effort, and over-all ability to stick at the MLB level.

"There is such a *long* way to go before we are ready to project this kind of prospect. The scout cannot really focus until high school, where he begins to see the athlete compete against better talent [all the athletes get better across the board, just because they've been playing for so long at this point]. Then the projection period starts to shorten and is against consistently better players. We will be striving to project just to find 'average' or better. Now not every player will hit .270 in MLB. Intangibles can help a kid become an overachiever. Don't ever take the dream away from the player who wants to be in the 7%!"

That's what it takes.

There is so much time involved, so many games to play, so many hits to make, so many batters to get out… it just isn't worth it if it isn't *fun*.

Even in the majors, your schedule lasts from April to (hopefully) October and spans 162 games, and that's just in the regular season. That is a long, long haul if you're only in it for the money. Baseball better be fun if you're going to be doing it that much, and it isn't fun if you get burned out on it early.

The Sandlot is for dreamers, and it's time to just enjoy the ride.

Remember when I said Gary is a parent? Listen to him talk from the gut:

"My son Chris played baseball. It never was a concern of mine that he would be a big league baseball player. I figured out quick that he would be better off to have a positive experience in athletics. To this day he thanks me. Chris was his class president in High School. He knows athletics played a great role in his leadership skills.

"It was difficult at times for me as a dad to step back and stay out of what my kids wanted to do. But I knew it was best, and I worked hard to support them in whatever they wanted to do. Once they charted their course, I supported them and helped them as best I could. It was *my* challenge as well as theirs, and they thanked me for it."

Listen to your kids and they'll thank you.

Those odds are in your favor.

CHAPTER 7

BUILDING BLOCKS FOR GUARANTEED SUCCESS AS A KEEPER OF THE SANDLOT

"BUILDER OR WRECKER"
(READ BY CHUCK SWINDOLL ON INSIGHT FOR LIVING)

I saw them tearing a building down, a group of men in a busy town,
With a hefty blow and a zesty yell, they swung with zest, and a side wall
fell.

Asked of the foreman, "Are these men skilled? The kind you would hire
if you had to build?"
He looked at me and laughed, "No, indeed. Unskilled labor is all I need.
Why they can wreck in a day or two what it has taken builders years to
do."

I asked myself as I went my way, "Which of the roles have I tried to
play?
Am I a builder with rule and square measuring and constructing with
skill and care?
Or am I a wrecker who walks the town intent with the business of tearing
down?"

Chapter Seven: Building Blocks for Guaranteed Success as a Keeper of the Sandlot

My road to success is paved with the investments of countless teachers, coaches, counselors, friends, and my parents. As I put together this book, I decided to seek out some of my old coaches and an old friend who've all gone as high in baseball as they wanted to go: my coach at the University of Oklahoma, Coach Enos Semore, who is in the College Coaches Hall of Fame; Gene Stephenson, coach of the Wichita State University Shockers and currently the second all-time winningest coach in college baseball, who was an assistant coach when I played at OU; and Ned Yost, Manager of the Kansas City Royals, who was one of my best friends as we toiled in triple-A ball.

Their desire to help you and me, parents and coaches and teachers and Keepers alike has driven this project.

This is required learning for all Keepers.

Coach Enos Semore

"If you can get your coaches to understand how great their responsibilities are, and the 'impact,' whether good or bad... that everything he does or says...will have on a kid, you will have done a great thing. I cannot tell you how many times a former player or coach has come back to me twenty, thirty, forty or fifty years later and *leveled* me with something I said or did, good or bad, that I didn't even realize I had done or said.

"Tell your coaches they are a greater influence than they will ever realize. You just cannot imagine what your actions and words will mean for a very long time."

"If I had it to do over again, I would take each player and coach individually aside and tell them how glad I was to have them in our program. I would do it every year. Do not assume anything. I would not leave it to them to just know and assume that I loved them."

I asked him about burnout, and he said this: "Realize that kids do not get 'burned out' on baseball. They get sick and tired of being harassed and yelled at every time they make a mistake. When a kid gets his butt kicked for every single mistake he makes, he will quit because he just hates it with everything in his body."

What about coaching? "Here are the life lessons you teach and how you make players great—this can start simply in the sandlot:

1. Be a good listener.
2. Make sure they understand that every time they practice and do something, they need to do it the right way.
3. You cannot be short on effort. Put forth the effort with all of the passion you have. Strive to be the best every day.
4. If you want to be great, make a list of the things you need to work on. Get faster, lose weight, change habits, and such. If you will not do this, you are just *dreaming* about being a great player.
5. Not everyone will *pay the price*. This is the key.
6. If you do not have a burning in your chest, leave. You have to have passion.
7. Don't accept excuses. Parents get mad their kids are not starting because they feel it reflects on them. Don't accept it.
8. Demanding effort and the consequences are imperative. We had a freshman All-American named Mike, and he had a tendency to hesitate for a split-second on pop-ups in foul territory. I told him, if he continued to do that he would hear from me in a big way, and it got to the point that I told Mike if he did it again, he would not start the next game. It happened again. And the next game was the first game of the College World Series. I tried to bring Mike along but he did it again, so I did what I said I would do. If I don't, then who am I? This is about raising young men.
9. Set expectations and follow them. The follow-through is hard, but it's important.
10. Stay calm. If you are calm, you can see it all while everyone else is going crazy. Those who get real high on a good play and real low on a bad play cannot win consistently.

"This is how I coached; this is who I am."

Gene Stephenson

Gene Stephenson is a winner. He has compiled an incredible list of accomplishments throughout a storied career as the Coach of the Wichita State University Shockers. But to me, he was "The General," our assistant coach at Oklahoma, who taught us how to play as a team. We were never "his" players. It was always about "us" or "we." We did it all as a team.

Here is the truth as he sees it:

1. "You must always realize that it is not about you. It is about *us*. The focus is on 'we' and 'us.' Whether it is your family or team, it is always about 'us.' You can't play [for me] if you don't care about the team as a whole. I am protective of kids' feelings, and I always tell my kids to go home and hug their parents. Be thankful for them. You want to talk about fundamentals? Start with these.

2. "You have to like yourself and have a great sense of who you are. Whether you are a player or coach, how you perceive yourself is integral to your success. If you are going to have any chance of winning, you have to surround yourself with good people and be one yourself. You win with people. It's all about people. Coaches and scouts are always looking for good people.

4. "Challenge your players to…
   - Be the best player/pitcher they can be.
   - Be the best student they can be.
   - Be the best son or daughter they can be.

These 3 things need to be burned into your player's heads from their first day on the Sandlot. It's easily taught and makes sense to everyone. Gene's three-step approach was used on me.

A. "Find some good in each kid. Praise him for what he does well. Kids always want to hear something good about themselves. Heck, we all do. But we are talking specifically about kids. When you do this,

"You know how to make anyone feel great even when they are not doing great."

Alex
Mustangs 1B/OF

58

he will come back to you for more. You get his attention with praise.

B. "Identify what needs to be worked on, especially the weaknesses, and start to make him complete. Teach your players the reason for working on weaknesses, although they may not fully understand yet. Who likes to work on the things we are not good at? We just want to do what's fun. They'll thank you for it down the road. Your weaknesses will get you beat, so even the 'best' work on their weaknesses continually.

"You made me love the game even more than I already did."

Alex
Mustangs 1B/OF

C. "Finish with the good. Give the assurance that hard work will pay off. Give them Hope. It is a great thing to give a kid. *Always* give hope

4. "Motivation comes from within. You must have the 'Separator.' The will to win is great, but the Separator is the commitment to *prepare* to win. If you ask anyone if they have the will to win, they will usually say, 'of course!' But in reality, not nearly as many have the desire or commitment to put in the time to prepare to win. I will always prefer the kid who has the desire to *prepare* to win and the fire in his gut to work hard enough to do it.

"I just loved it when you would tell me my stuff was really working when I was pitching."

Brennan
Mustangs P/3B

5. "Dream big. Take on the giants. Go for it and don't be afraid of defeat. Encourage kids to take chances at practice. They will learn what they can get away with. Of course, you must further coach them in situations where chances can be taken and where they can't, this is life.

6. "Make preparation a habit.

7. "It's never about talent. The measure of a truly great player or coach is the one who pays attention to the

detail and works on the things that he does not do well.

8. "Good luck versus bad luck. Here is a big one. The difference is simply this. You must have the ability and determination to overcome adversity. No matter who you are, you are going to someday face some serious trials. They will happen to everyone. How you react to these trials will determine whether or not you win.

9. "If your kid gets through the whole process and maze of athletics and still loves baseball, that will be wonderful. Know that there are many coaches who will seek out and find the gifted athlete with that burning desire and will to prepare and give him a chance. If a kid has that kind of talent, the coaches are going to want him. Ultimately in all of life, the ones who prepare are the ones who always seem to be the 'luckier' ones.

10. "Finally, remember that all of these points build on each other. Your legacy is truly what you give to others. Starting specifically in the playground of life and traveling all the way to the top, your legacy will be something you said or did to make someone's world a better place."

Ned Yost

As my buddy Ned Yost and I talked at length about the developmental years of the Sandlot, he said something that I have not been able to get out of my head. "Billy, player development does not happen at [the major league] level. It happens when children are five or six years old and they learn how to play fearlessly and develop their natural talents."

Like a bolt out of the blue Ned went straight to the heart of what one of our prime goals should be in the early years. The excitement of the first few years of little league and kids' sports are just that, pure excitement and chaos. Everyone can tell the stories of running around the bases the wrong way, the constant pointing, chanting, cheering and yelling at everything. It is a great time.

What 22 years of coaching has shown me is that all of the worrying and fretting and anxious moments that we all share about our children's futures in baseball are largely unnecessary. (Of course, this is much easier said than done, because there are just times we have to worry like crazy, we're parents!) Ned pointed out in his own special way that this should be a time where each child is allowed to develop what comes naturally to him. Each kid is special and has natural talents.

(A quick aside: I once received a call from a reporter from the *Kansas City Star* who wanted to interview my players for an article, and that he'd buy the pizza. Well, what a day. The interview went well, especially when he asked the question, "What is your favorite sport?" I started to swell up with pride when most of them yelled, "Baseball, of course!" But then Wylie looked at him, raised his hand, and said, "Whatever sport we're playing." The whole team yelled with approval, and I remembered that not everyone will play baseball forever. Some of my kids left sports to play music, go into acting, join the debate team—there are plenty of other worthwhile pursuits.)

One of the really great gifts you can give a child is the time and encouragement needed to develop their strengths and true talents. When you look at your first team of six- and seven-year-olds, you aren't looking just at kids: you're also looking at future doctors, teachers, coaches, engineers, bankers, salesmen, CEOs, COOs, Presidents of big companies, entrepreneurs… the list goes on.

So set up these early years as a fun time to develop natural abilities. Your parents and their kids will love it and appreciate it. You don't have to yell because your future engineer can't hit his cut-off man at age eight.

Your strategy is to take a bunch of your kid's friends and their parents and gradually make them look like a baseball team (to the kids, that is). Trust me, the best times as a community will happen just because you know this and got it right.

Set the expectation early. Challenge *your* coaching abilities to making this collection of friends a cohesive good team. *You* accept the responsibility of setting the bar and include everyone in the fun.

I always had the goal of making it work with what I had. Playing the cards I was dealt. We had to live together for a long time, might as well play together, right?

Realize that how they handle their future roles as athletes, students, parents and work in their chosen field will be molded under your watch. This is a huge responsibility.

They will either be confident, secure, team players, risk-takers, empathetic, caring leaders *or* fearful, insecure, selfish, scared of their shadows, and basically impossible-to-deal-with people.

Another huge thing for Ned is to teach your kids how to play fearlessly. Either they learn to play the game well and live life to the fullest with *no fear* or they will become *fearful* kids who never reach their potential because they're scared of being harassed and yelled at.

You cannot reach your potential in anything if you are afraid. And if you get yelled at every time you make a mistake, you're going to play fearfully.

If there is one emotion that everyone has to face and conquer it is fear. Parents, coaches, players all have to learn how to conquer their fears.

Fear of striking out.

Fear of getting hit by the pitch.

Fear of failure.

Fear of losing the game for your team.

Fear of not making the team.

Fear makes cowards of us all.

I have talked to hundreds of people from all walks of life who quit little league and gave up the game because they hated getting yelled at every time they made a mistake. Yelling made them afraid. You can just see the depth of the disappointment when they tell me that.

You can see the hurt and there is no doubt about who it was who made them give up the game.

My dear friend, Kevin Seitzer, currently the hitting coach for the Atlanta Braves, says it as simply as can be. "Never be the coach who makes a kid give up the game."

Without a doubt, the single most important key to success and reaching your full God given potential is cutting loose and learning to play the game without fear. The truth is, failure is just part of the process of preparing for victory somewhere down the road.

John Mason, in his book *An Enemy Called Average* states, "How we respond to failure and mistakes is one of the most important decisions we make every day." And then he says, "Failure doesn't mean that nothing has been accomplished. There is always the opportunity to learn something. What is in you will always be bigger than whatever is around you."

You have to have courage as a coach in order to give courage to your players. You cannot give what you do not have. Have the courage to give it.

We all face stresses, the kids will have plenty of stresses in their lives. Normal stresses for children are tough enough much less additional stresses put on them from athletics, parents and especially their peers.

Stresses cause kids to break.

But a confident coach who allows his kids to fail and cheers them on to keep up the fight will be the one that leads them to being great players, happy kids, and successful adults. You *have* to be confident. Do not *ever* show up your players. Help them play fearlessly.

We all have experienced the moment when we are playing fearlessly and the juices are flowing. You can hold nothing back and achieve greatness. Hesitation kills.

My friend Lee Roberts used to encourage, "Take a swing! That's what baseball is for!" You're never going to get on base if you don't swing.

Teach your kids to swing.

And don't be afraid, yourself. You can't fool kids—they know if you believe in yourself or not. And they love it when you are human. They love to forgive. They especially love it when you tell them you messed up and they get to tell you, "It's okay."

Never be so confident that you don't apologize and ask your kids' forgiveness when you blow it (and trust me, you *will* blow it). Don't be so hard on yourself; we've all been there. We're just members of a fraternity of parents and coaches—Keepers—who have put it on the line to coach.

CHAPTER 8

RELEASING YOUR KIDS

"WITHOUT A DOUBT, THE GIRLS I COACHED WHOSE PARENTS RELEASED THEM TO THE GAME ACHIEVED AT THE HIGHEST LEVEL."

LANE GREEN
DIRECTOR OF DISTRICT ATHLETICS & ACTIVITIES
FOR OLATHE DISTRICT SCHOOLS
OLATHE, KS

Little league is fun, but eventually your players will grow up and the real world will creep into their world. My friend Lane Green was a girls' varsity basketball coach for 11 years and has served as a high school athletic director for the past 14 years, currently at Olathe North High School, an athletic powerhouse in Kansas. He told me about some of the girls he coached who were absolutely livid when the basketball team cuts were announced and some of the friends were not on the roster. One of them who played in four NCAA tournaments and the final four in 2002 for the University of Oklahoma was one of the most determined, competitive and hard working athletes who ever played for Lane. Nevertheless, Lane describes her as having difficulty accepting the cuts that had happened to her friends.

Even though she realized all her friends would not go to the next level, and it was inevitable that they wouldn't, the realization of this separation was painful for her to accept. To children, their friends are a significant part of their self-worth.

While the eventual separation is evident to most parents, coaches, and, let's call it the Establishment, for the lack of a better word, it is *never* evident or easy for kids to accept the separation from their friends. That's why the Sandlot years are so special.

This is also why I try to prepare all my kids for the high school level and experience. Until then, it should all be fun and instructional.

Lane Green shared with me a conversation that he had with Bruce Brown while driving him to a speaking engagement in the spring of 2007. Bruce Brown is the Director of ProActive Coaching and the NAIA Special Presenter for the Champions of Character program. The author of numerous books, Bruce Brown worked for over 35 years as a teacher, coach and athletic administrator at the junior high, high school and collegiate levels.

During their conversation, he described to Lane the four stages of coaching: The joy stage, the technical stage, the competitive stage followed by the master stage.

1. **The Joy Stage.** This is the Sandlot. Elementary school through eighth grade.

2. **The Instructional Stage.** This happens at the same time.
3. **The Competitive Stage.** This starts around twelve to thirteen years old and goes into high school.
4. **The Master Stage.** College and the pros.

Personally, I believe it needs to be fun in each stage. And not just fun, but it needs to get even *more* fun as you get older. It better be really fun once you get to stages three and four, because you are about to eat, sleep, and breathe the game at that point—you better enjoy it.

So, with that in mind, here are *my* four stages of fun:

1. **Fun to be a kid.** Play with your friends. Have fun at school, at practice, during games, going over to your friends' houses.

   "There were so many fun and funny times."

   David
   Mustangs P/OF

2. **Fun learning the game.** Here you begin to compete and see what it means to win and enjoy doing so as a part of a team. My buddy, Gary with the Cardinals says the scouts don't really care until a kid reaches sixteen or seventeen, but my experience is that something in athletes kicks in around twelve or thirteen that says, *Hey, I kind of like this. Let's throw some wood on this fire.* Winning and losing starts to affect players at this age. It's still fun and still full of friends, but something starts going on that is really cool here.

3. **Fun making the high school team.** Fun that comes from committing to what you are really good at. To be able to make a team because you work hard, practice hard, have the ability to compete with the best around, and work every day to get better. Fun to start to identify your weaknesses and work diligently at them to become a complete player. Your strengths are not good enough to carry you if you have significant weaknesses. The competition will now identify your weaknesses and exploit them. You will be eaten alive as the competition heats up. This needs to be *fun* to you. Your parents are

no longer around to help you, think for you, cover up for you, be your advocate. You have now moved to the Competitive stage. Hard work will be required of you every single day. You better know how to motivate yourself to do this to. And you better still think this constant drive to get better is *fun*.

4. **Fun to compete for your meals.** The pros, where it's fun to compete to take another guy's living from him. Fun to play under the relentless pressure of no mistakes. You are expected to have "mastered" everything it requires to play at the highest level. The competition is relentless and fierce, but you can still have fun all the way through. Trust me, if it isn't fun, you won't be able to play it the way it needs to be played.

· · · · · ·

Lane went on to talk about something very important in the Sandlot: "Without a doubt, the girls I coached whose parents *released* them to the game achieved at the highest level. They played with *reckless abandon*. Not always the most talent, but they played their hearts out. They left nothing on the floor."

I cannot state this enough: kids must learn to play fearlessly, to leave it all on the floor (or field), to play their hearts out.

Let them play free of worry. And parents, Keepers, learn to release your kids. If they are going to make it in anything, they have to be willing to take chances, fail, and be unafraid to try.

Confident parents raise confident kids, so have confidence in your kids and in the other parents and Keepers around you: release your kids to the game.

Release your kids from the pressure.

Release your kids from the unrealistic expectations.

Release your kids from fear of failure.

Release your kids from the constant harassment to exceed

and always win at all costs.
Release your kids to play the game.
Release them when they are ready to fly.
Release them confident.
And they will always come back.

"You taught us to play the game. The memories of these seasons will stick with me forever."
Paul
Mustangs P/1B

. . . . . .

You know what phrase I hear that all the time? "We just want the kids to have fun." So many coaches use this catch-all phrase as a justification for hidden agendas and insecurities, turning what should be a great childhood experience into a military exercise that kids quickly grow tired of.

How many coaches say they "just want the kids to have fun" while also barking out phrases like:

"Everybody over here and be quiet!"

"If you all don't pay attention, we're going to run until you do!"

"You don't win because you don listen!"

"We're going to have to split the team up because some aren't as good as others and it isn't fair to the ones who want more."

On and on and on.

Have you ever asked an elementary school kid his ideas on fun? I will guarantee you that 90% of the time his answer will be along these lines: "To be with my friends, not worry about winning every game, and not getting yelled at."

Most of the time, the answer will stop with, "Just being with my friends."

Believe me, I have tried with everything I can imagine to get a kid to say, "Winning is the most important thing for me." You know why? Because I'm an adult—that's what *I* think is the most important. I have been programmed that winning is the only thing, that's why we keep score, it's the American way, there are only two kinds of people, winners and losers, first place and last, on and on and on...

Well, that's why we have to keep the Sandlot free. It is the only time where little kids are free to be kids. They don't care about or even understand your silly agenda.

I have been lucky to have some of the greatest assistant coaches and have witnessed some of the greatest coaching jobs by just regular Joes like me who continually do an unbelievable job of letting the boys play. It is easy to say you want them to have fun; it is another thing to have the guts and brains and confidence to *let* them have fun.

Trust me, I have had to endure with my little leaguers an occasional assistant that could absolutely *not* accept the fact that the boys needed to have this fun time and that *everything* needed to be run their way and that was it. If that's you, Keeper, you need to wise up. Their speeches, tirades, sarcastic remarks, constant diatribes about missing a cut-off man, not tagging up, not blocking a ball, not getting their glove down... it was all unbearable.

I remember one of my little leaguers staring at one of my assistants during one of his "speeches" and I could almost hear him say to himself, "How stupid do you think we are?" And meanwhile, the kid of the dad who was beating us all up with his rants was clearly uncomfortable and would have crawled under a rock if possible. *Kids hate it when their parents make fools out of themselves in front of their friends.*

Yours truly is no exception, I have had my moments. During a state play-off game, a couple of our players had been tagged out by an over-zealous shortstop with what I really thought was excessive force. Their first baseman had stuck his knee out and really stuck it to one of our runners going by first base.

I called time out, walked out to the umpire in the field and asked him if he was watching this physical attack on our base-runners. He gave me a stone-faced look, I didn't know what had registered, if anything, and he told me he was fully aware of the situation. The other team's coaches were acting oblivious to this, so I guess they were just being cool to it or oblivious themselves to the potential dangers of the head-hunting sweep tags by their shortstop.

A few plays later, the same thing happened and I again went out to challenge the umpire, and all of a sudden I hear, "You're gone!" From the home plate umpire, no less.

"For what?" I asked

"You crossed the line!"

"Which line?"

"The third-base foul line! You crossed it to argue, and so you're gone!"

The point of this story is that on the way home, Will, then thirteen, asked, "Why did you get thrown out of the game?" I immediately went into the whole story of injuries to our team, taking up for our players, and so on.

"Yeah, Dad, but why did you get thrown out of the game?"

It hit me like a ton of bricks. I had crossed several lines.

First, I crossed a literal line.

Second, when I got thrown out, I crossed the line that a Keeper should not cross with his team—I left them to fend for themselves.

Third, I crossed the line of discipline and self-control.

I had not handled the situation well at all. Nobody gained anything from me getting thrown out. I should have stopped the game until someone running the tournament fixed the problem. I had choices. It would have been easy. It would have been better. It would have stayed inside the line.

Don't cross the line.

Kids hate it when parents cross the line and act nuts. They just cannot understand why *we* have to be so bizarre. Again, if you get out of the dugout and listen to your kids, you can really begin to experience once again the joy of the Sandlot and be thankful they have let you back into that time you had of being a kid.

Now, I have actually coached a kid whose dad would yell at him while he batted, and the kid could yell back just fine. It was great—just the way their relationship worked. Actually, Carter could hit better with his dad there and yelling; he was almost lost when his dad *wasn't* there, so his mom would yell, and if she wasn't there, his sister would take it up. Carter had to have someone from his family yelling at him. "Carter, keep your elbow up!" "It *is* up! I can't get it any higher!" Just hilarious.

I am also amazed at the guys who can yell so much, be the center of attention, scream at kids… and they themselves probably couldn't hit a lick. Now I don't think you have to be in the Hall of Fame to be a coach, far from it, most of us aren't, but it is harder than you think, and you should know that hitting a baseball is tough for even the best to do. Remember what we talked about earlier: failing only 70% of the time (i.e. hitting .300) is considered great.

You really want the kids to have fun? Find out what *they* would like to do while they are in their Sandlot years, make the game really fun and provide a format for them to do so. Let them make some calls, laugh with them, bring your smile, and check your ego at the door. Leave your tie in the car *with your cell phone.* Don't bring that thing into the Sandlot—that belongs in the real world.

You will never regret loosening up and allowing yourself to go back to the Sandlot with your kid. It can be just as good for you as it once was, probably better, because it is your kid. Nothing is better than when our kids have success—it's what we all want. We just have to measure success in what they all become, ballplayers or not, and ultimately when they thank us for being there and encouraging them all the way.

Again, Joe Simpson said, "If you will listen to your kids, they will tell you where they want to go. We just enjoyed the ride."

CHAPTER 9

THE COACH'S KID

"HEY DAD, THE GUYS WANT TO KNOW IF SATURDAY MORNING COULD JUST BE A FUN SCRIMMAGE, NO PRACTICE, JUST PLAY. I TOLD THEM I'D TALK TO YOU, CAN WE JUST SCRIMMAGE? HOOVIE SAYS HIS MOM WILL BRING DONUTS."

DREW SEVERNS
AGE 11

Dad,

I have been so fortunate over these first 15 years of my life to have you as a coach and a father. The way you have been so patient and helping over all these years really means a lot to me and my friends. I have so many times looked at the other kids with their coaches and thinking, "Those kids have no idea." What I mean by that is there isn't one kid that has experienced or learned more from their coach than what I have learned from you. Everything you have said to me over the years I have taken to heart and I know one day my kids will too. I know that everybody on our team has been blessed to have had you coach our team throughout our little league years and I know everyone will never forget any of the moments. I have two favorite moments with you over my years; the first one is our car rides to and from ball games.

I will never forget some of the conversations we've had coming home from 3&2. I will miss those the most because I could never get tired of you telling me how good I am :). I will never meet anyone else in my whole life that knows more about baseball than you, and just to be in your presence just teaching me and encouraging me about the game is something I'll never forget.

My other favorite memory is probably the most important of all. Just playing catch with you. Now this one I know will not end. Whether it was at the club or in our front yard, I got to experience something so great which a lot of boys my age don't get to experience, spending time with your dad. Sure most of the time playing catch was to get me ready for Tuesday night's game, or the State Tournament, but every time you and I would grab our mitts and throw a ball, I could not have been happier just to cherish time with you.

So dad I want to thank you so much from all my years with you. You have transformed me and 12 of my best friends over the years from kids, to great ballplayers that will never forget the times of little league. You have made my childhood so much more enjoyable and I know that I will never forget the years that you were a great coach, but more importantly, and incredible father.

Love,
Your 401(k)
Will Severns

CHAPTER NINE: THE COACH'S KID

How many of you are coaching your kid? I mean your own child? Do these kids deserve their own chapter or what?

I could not and would not have written this book if my boys had not pushed me to do it. Matthew, Drew and Will. My sons. My gifts. And as important as they are, I *really* wouldn't have moved forward without my daughter, Sarah, telling me, "Dad, who's been doing it longer than you and knows more about it than you?" In other words, "Daddy, you are really pretty old and you need to get it done."

I am honored and humbled that my "trophies" have played the game, continue to play the game and still love the game with great passion.

So, here are some tips that will make you a great coach.

(And I know that many of you are coaching your own daughters, but I only coached my sons, so I think of coaching my kids in terms of boys. Don't get mad when I keep writing "him" and "he" about coaching your own kids—it applies to daughters, too.)

If you are coaching your kid, treat him like he is your most valuable bench coach. Listen to him. He is the heartbeat of your team. He knows what your team is saying, thinking, what they want. Listen to him.

He is the lightning rod for everything, and it is a huge, extra load for him to carry. Remember that.

He knows who is happy and sad.

He knows where *you* are coming up short, from the uniform colors and design to playing time to problems at home or school the boys are having. He is inevitably the one who gets unloaded on.

He is a tremendous asset to you. Your child is a "Keeper" in his own way.

He will fight for his friends and, if you are sensitive to him, he will help you get the most out of your team.

Listening to my sons has always kept me out of a lot of trouble. If I was questioning a kid's ability and desire to play, inevitably my boys would get right to the point and set me straight on the whole picture as to where this kid fit in. Hear me when I say this: *they were never wrong.*

I feel sorry for the guys who coach their sons and never take full advantage of this. I know I didn't for a long time.

Poor coach's sons have to listen to the whole deal. All the ranting and raving. They deserve trophies just for that.

Of course, being the coach's son did get some advantages. For example, my sons were always the first to know if practice was cancelled or if a game was rained out. (Just kidding.)

When it comes to playing time, you have to know that your kids want their friends to play equally. This should not be a problem if you are understanding what kids want. Kids honestly don't want to be in there every inning at the expense of their friends. (If they do, they're being bratty and don't deserve the extra playing time anyway.)

I could really see this when I was contemplating the ride out to a game. I would ask my sons which game or time during the game they wanted to sit. We would talk through the game and what the possibilities might be, and, for example, Matthew would say, "I want to sit out the first four innings of the first game and *if* you need me to pinch run or play defense, you can put me in around the fifth inning. I really want to play the night game."

Now Matthew grew up and made the All Johnson County Baseball Team his Senior year, then played four years of college baseball at Taylor University in Indiana. The boy wanted to play *all the time.* But he also wanted his friends to play, and to make sure he was just like everyone else. Being treated equal is real important to most kids.

Kids just want to be in the mix. They really hate to get singled out, and coach's kids are no different.

Now the real benefit for you, Keeper, is that everybody loves it when the coach's kid *doesn't* start every game. It takes a ton of pressure off of you, your kid, the other parents, the other players. Everybody is happy because you're being *fair*!

It's great!

You have to treat everyone equally. Kids love this, and your own kids will help you figure this out.

One other subtle advantage that comes from being the

Keeper is being able to sit kids at the same time that are really close friends. Make it easier. Sometimes it may be your two best players, but that really works to your advantage. It shows that you aren't playing favorites and sends the message to everyone that you think *each* kid on the team can get the job done.

That is a great message! I always told my kids, "Sooner or later during the season, it will come down to *you*. You need to be ready, and I have complete confidence that you will be ready to perform and get the job done." By not playing favorites, you're backing up that message.

(I have also thought that during this time on the bench, if they want to run and get a coke or something, let them. We never lost a game because two kids on the bench were off getting a coke or going to the bathroom.)

Don't be afraid to take the pressure off. It ultimately pays off because they get hungry to get back in the game. Most do, anyway.

One final thought on coaches and their sons: you are going to need a bunch of help. There are usually several parents that can help you and would love to be asked.

The more parents you get involved in your team, the better.

I will forever be indebted to the assistant coaches who helped me be a good coach.

Before every practice, Lee would have the bases set and a jug of lemonade hanging from the backstop...the best!

Rob would arrive early and get the whiffle ball batting practice going. The kids loved Rob and he could really get a team swinging.

Brad would get the starting pitcher ready and make sure our catcher was ready and his gear was in place. It didn't hurt that his son *was* the catcher.

Paul would hit outfield flies, and his son Johnny would catch in for him. At times I wanted him to play, but he was seven years younger than the other kids on the team.

I would hit infield if I felt like it, and wait on the opposing scorekeeper to start badgering me for the line-up, a ritual I detested.

Thanks for all your help, fellas.

• • • • • •

Okay, one more thing: I have never been a yeller.

Kids play better with a routine, just like professional and college players do.

I am glad I have never been a yeller.

Whenever I heard an opposing coach threatening and yelling that his twelve-year-olds better get going or there is going to be heck to pay, I always knew we had a good chance to get 'em early.

CHAPTER 10

WHAT'S A PARENT TO DO?

"TO THE BEST OF YOUR ABILITY, BE THERE."

COACH SEVERNS

"MAKE SURE YOUR KIDS HAVE FUN. TELL YOUR PARENTS TO RELAX AND ENJOY THEIR KIDS. PUTTING UNDUE PRESSURE ON CHILDREN TO PLAY ANY SPORTS IS A HUGE MISTAKE."

GARY LaROCQUE
ST. LOUIS CARDINALS

"THERE ARE 2 THINGS YOU NEED TO GET RIGHT IN THE EARLY YEARS. LET EACH CHILD DEVELOP THEIR NATURAL ABILITIES AND TEACH THEM TO PLAY FEARLESSLY."

NED YOST#
Ndqvdv#Flwl#r|dov

"TALK TO YOUR KIDS. RIGHT OUT OF THE WOMB, TALK TO YOUR KIDS."

DICK KRAMER
PRINCIPAL, SHAWNEE MISSION NORTH HIGH SCHOOL

CHAPTER TEN: WHAT'S A PARENT TO DO?

As a parent, it's tough when your child encounters the inevitable rough seas of sports. And those rough seas will come. You can't protect your child forever—they will encounter a coach they don't get along with, or they'll make a mistake that loses the game, or they'll want to blame one of their *friends* for making a mistake that loses the game... the list goes on and on.

What do you do? Where do you go?

It's really gut-wrenching. If I told you it was easy, I'd be lying.

But...

You and your child will make it through. I speak from experience, because each of my sons went through serious challenges that almost killed me. And we made it.

I have had many parents, friends, coaches, and people ask me how I have remained so cool all of these years, but these parents, friends, coaches, and people just haven't seen my bad days. Hey, we all have bad days. No one is always cool. We are parents, though, and we do have to keep things under control. If we don't, who will?

As a parent and as a Keeper, you just have to realize that one of your key roles in life is to teach your children how to keep fighting, to deal with adversity, and to face the challenges of life head-on. As one of my friends, Bill Bade, says, "In the end, it's not only the things we've done for our children, but what we've taught them to do for themselves that will help them become successful human beings."

Worrying will not help.

When your children and team see worry on your face, *they* will start to worry. And if you spend all of your time worrying about the future, you're going to miss out on the present—you'll miss the experience of your child growing up.

Childhood is too short to spend it worrying. That goes both for your kids and for you. If you approach difficulties with guidance and a steady hand, your kids will learn how to handle it. All you have to do is just be there.

You cannot predict or control the future. But you can sure

teach your kid how to deal with adversity and overcome tough times and accomplish his or her dreams.

You have no idea what your child may ultimately want to do, or even if it is in sports. They're playing in the Sandlot because their friends are there—it doesn't matter the sport; your kid really just wants to be with their friends.

In fourth grade, Matthew came to me and said those dreaded words, "Dad, I don't think I want to play baseball this year." Made me swallow my gum.

I said, "Well, buddy that's fine, if it's really what you think, okay." I didn't really mean it. Here I was, a former baseball player, and coach of Matthew's baseball team—baseball was my life, and I wanted my boy to keep going in it. I wanted to take hold of both of his shoulders and say, "No way! Baseball's the best—why would you give that up?" I wanted to make him play.

Instead, I just held my tongue and let him make his choices.

Fortunately, as spring got closer and Matthew's friends started talking about baseball, he rallied and came to his senses (just kidding [kind of]) and chose to play baseball. Although it's hard sometimes, you have to keep from overreacting.

Matthew worked hard to get a starting spot on his high school team, and as he headed into his junior year of high school, he was slated to be the center fielder. He came home one day and said, "Dad, there is a new kid in school. Everyone says he plays center field, *and* is a pitcher, and that he's great. He's living with one of the assistant baseball coaches. What do you think about that?"

Quietly, I about lost it. This can be a problem in high school athletics. Recruiting isn't allowed, but when a kid has a lot of promise and talent, some coaches find ways around the restrictions against recruiting. This kid's family didn't live in our district, so he shouldn't have been allowed to play for our team, but since he was living with one of the coaches, he was now technically living in the district, and therefore allowed to play. There was nothing I could do about it.

Matthew had worked hard, waited his turn, and now someone had deliberately moved a kid into the district and jeopardized Matthew's spot on the team.

That's what I *thought*. But here's what I *said* to Matthew:

"Well, buddy, there is always a great chance that someone will move into the neighborhood and challenge you for your position, so go beat him out. I know you can do it."

What else could I say? I had to have faith. I had to give Matthew confidence. I surely could not change anything; this new kid was living with a coach, for crying out loud!

I didn't want Matthew to worry all school year long until baseball season started so I painted the picture that at least the *team* would be better with this great new addition, and maybe they would win State. And if this kid *was* a great pitcher, Matthew could play probably play center field while the new kid pitched the championship game.

Turns out this new kid didn't adjust to the school well and only lasted half the season. Matthew moved over to center field, added some beef to his frame, kept playing, had a great senior season, made the All-County, Conference, and District teams, and went on to play in college.

As a parent, you just need to be there. That is what a parent has to do: be there and give your kid an anchor.

The point of the Sandlot is that your kids need to have fun and prepare for the challenges. All of the coaches at the highest levels and scouts of the pros will tell you that they need to have fun, learn, develop their skills, and play the game fearlessly, nothing else.

I am convinced that Matthew learned how to face his giants at an early age, how to calmly go about his business with confidence, and that helped him in this situation. Now, he is in the business world and doing the same thing, taking on the challenges of work and raising a family.

Our next child, Drew, played in a really rough situation for a coach who was very difficult. This coach had all kinds of issues, and so consequently, high school baseball was exceptionally difficult at times for Drew and his teammates.

On one particularly ugly trip out of town, the team fell apart. It was a mess. Everyone fell apart. I wound up driving back home with a van load of seven players who just wanted to be consoled. It was absolutely horrible.

The next night, around two in the morning, I was sound asleep when I felt this huge presence hovering over me. It was Drew. I reached around his massive shoulders and pulled him close. All of a sudden the tears started flowing down my shoulders and back. My bed was soaked.

My son was broken. His heart was broken. Even as I type this, remembering it, my heart is pounding.

Anybody who tells you this is easy is nuts.

Right then, in the middle of the night, I wanted to call the coach and ask him if he would like to share this moment.

I held my tongue and encouraged Drew in the best way I knew how just to keep playing and not to let this coach be the coach that drove him to give up the game. This coach had his own issues, and I knew that if Drew just kept playing, he would find joy in the game again. It was going to get better.

Well, it didn't get any better until the coach resigned. Even then, it still didn't get much better, but the boys made it through.

Keeper, grab hold of this thought. Learn how to *respond* instead of *react* to these really tough conflicts. Teach your children the difference in the two.

As long as a kid has his friends and his parents, he will make it through.

I am glad to say that the coach fought his way through his issues and is doing good. It was very difficult, but the experience, although painful, made the kids tougher and drew them closer.

Drew went on to play out his remaining years of high school ball, and then four years in college, following his brother's footsteps at Taylor University. His resilience, tenacious spirit, love of the game, and fearless play are remarkable.

Let me make something clear, as far as this story is concerned: there is no room for abuse. Keeper, if you're abusing your kids verbally or physically, you need to stop. Now. Parents, if your children are playing for abusive coaches, get involved. Most coaches do it for the right reason, so if you can, offer to help. Be there. Stay close. Don't spend all of your time second-guessing from a distance. And talk to your kid.

As I listened to what my kids had to say, I realized they were doing all right. The problems they had were not as big to them as I saw them. They were fine. They just needed to know I was there with them. Be there.

Don't underestimate your kid. Kids are exceptionally insightful and smart.

Take Matthew, again. In high school, he was playing both basketball and baseball, but he knew he had to decide which one to focus on. His rationale: "You know, Dad, four hours of basketball practice for me is no longer fun. Four hours of baseball, I love."

Fun should always rule the day.

I sincerely enjoyed watching my kids grow and learn to stand on their own two feet. I am elated when I hear of the great accomplishments of the kids who played for me down the road. It comes with experience.

Trust me, they will be okay.

Kids have to navigate through their own world as best they can.

It can be cruel.

It is pressure-packed.

School is tough.

It's full of peer pressure.

The pounding is constant.

Kids can't please everybody, even us parents, all the time.

It will get to be too much if we don't give them great help.

The Sandlot should be their escape to play.

Let them have their Sandlot.

That's what you can do.

CHAPTER 11

MORE THAN A BASEBALL TEAM

CHAPTER ELEVEN: MORE THAN A BASEBALL TEAM

At breakfast one morning, I was talking with one of my friends and assistant coach Paul Black about our team as a community. "You know, Coach," he said, "we have done a great job here of parental management."

That was a term I had never heard, much less thought about.

Another great friend and coach, Steve Owens, talked about our team as a "great neighborhood team." We weren't the team that had held tryouts in an effort to find the best nine players—we just wanted great kids that would go through school together, and parents that loved to sit through the dog days of little league together.

In other words, we were in it for the long haul.

We taught everyone to get along. We made sure everyone was considered and that we paid attention to everyone's feelings. No one ever got thrown under the bus.

I always tried to be flexible with my team. If a kid wanted to play more baseball than we did, it was fine with me if he wanted to go to another team, as long as I was told he would be gone. At times it creates a few line-up changes and challenges, but there are always exceptions, and some kids truly want to play more, or their parents may want them to. If the boys are going to go to high school together, why would I want to make a big deal about it?

But on the whole, the Mustangs had more of a heart for each other than for the game. How could we not? We darn near lived together.

Paul said something else at that breakfast: "Where I am from in Iowa, we realize the fact that we will someday have to depend on our neighbors to help us out and maybe save our lives in a crisis. I call it the Iowa Fence Law—I cannot hate my neighbor. At best, I must tolerate him and figure out a way to get along."

What a lesson. If we ever pick an eleventh commandment, "I cannot hate my neighbor" would surely have my vote.

Yours truly was the recipient of the greatest life-saving gift from my team.

Over ten years ago, a routine physical check-up and a huge

stroke of luck uncovered a malignant melanoma behind my left ear. It was a Level Four melanoma, the worst possible, and was 3.2 centimeters deep. It was a near-death experience, but I got through it with a lot of prayer and some wonderful doctors removing it through surgery.

Afterward, my doctor wanted me to go to Duke University for four injections of radiated melanoma to help me fight off future problems. I booked a flight to Duke, got it all scheduled... and then my health insurance provider rejected the treatment because it wasn't approved by the FDA.

One of my Panther dads called to see when I was heading to Duke, and when I told him about my insurance problem, he instantly said, "Coach, don't even think about cancelling your flight."

"Bruce, it's not your problem," I said. "Don't worry about it, I'll get there." I didn't have the money to pay for the treatment, but I figured I'd get it somehow.

That night at practice, ten different families showed up and handed me envelopes full of money. Completely paid for everything. I was absolutely blown away that my parents would do that for me. Not that they weren't awesome to begin with; it was just family taking care of its own.

(I tell that story to show how the Prairie Panther families were in it for the long haul, and because it touches my heart to recount it, and also to say this: *please wear sunscreen*.)

Years later, the unthinkable happened...we lost a mom. The Mustang family was dealt a devastating blow.

One Sunday afternoon, just painting with her husband Walt and (as usual) getting things done, Donna died suddenly from a dissecting aneurysm. I received a terrible call that Donna was gone. I headed to the hospital and literally caught her son and husband in my arms as we all reeled from this horrific turn of events.

There is no way to describe the loss of Donna. How do you explain this kind of disaster? She was Walt's wife, a mom of three. She was the Mustangs scorekeeper, the *only* mom who knew what was going on during a baseball game.

Nobody ever thinks about this type of thing happening to

them. We surely didn't. Donna was so full of life. She had daycare in her home, taking care of other's kids along with her own. The cackling in the stands when Donna was holding court and teaching the other moms was at times hilariously distracting to a game. She coached her daughter's softball team and assisted the boys with their wrestling; even getting on the mat at times to make a point.

And all of a sudden, the Mustangs were learning the ultimate lesson about appreciating each other, loving your neighbors, and never assuming anything. As best we could, the family of the Mustangs joined the extended community and wrapped their arms around Walt and the kids. We knew we could never come close to being sufficient to meet the needs of the family or fill the hole that Donna left. But we were there.

Family, taking care of its own.

Walt wrote me an email sometime after: "First of all let me thank you and the Mustangs for all you have done for us. The Mustangs are so much more than a baseball team. They have been our support, anchors, and enablers during this time. Donna loved each Mustang, mother, dad, and family member. We will never be able to repay you all for the help you have given us during this extremely tough time. We will make it with your help. Thanks again, Walt and the kids."

Well Walt, according to Iowa Fence Law, some day we are going to need you right back. You will be there and we will be thankful.

Keepers, understand the bigger picture.

Everybody on the bus. It's a long ride.

CHAPTER 12

FORGIVEN

"IT'S OK COACH, YOU JUST HAD A BAD DAY."

CARTER
7TH GRADE DRAGONS

CHAPTER TWELVE: FORGIVEN

"If we confess our sins, He is faithful and just to forgive us our sins and to cleanse us from all unrighteousness." (1 John 1:9)

Confession is good for the soul.

Just like going to a baseball game, you think you have seen it all and something happens that you have never seen before.

None of us know it all or are anywhere near perfect. Therefore, the need for this chapter.

Needing forgiveness is a terrible feeling. Asking for it is a great one. Receiving it is even better.

Kids don't like it when you make a mistake, but they love it when you ask for forgiveness. They're the most forgiving creatures on the planet.

Good thing, because, Keeper, you're going to need it.

Don't be afraid to ask.

Don't be afraid to receive.

Every now and then I would have a conversation with a dad/coach that I was usually pretty close to and he would all of a sudden take our conversation to a deeper level.

I talk to a lot of dads, and I hear phrases like "I blew it," "I just couldn't handle it," and "I've cried myself to sleep over the way I treated my son." The internal struggle gets intense.

Sometimes I have surprised myself with my sense of self-control when dealing with ignorance or other coaches who seem to me to have little or no clue. But one day I *really* surprised myself, my team, and my parents.

During the heat of a tournament, we were playing horribly. Our opponents were about as unsportsmanlike as they could be, obnoxious, but a pretty sound team, fundamentally.

But man, were they obnoxious. And it was even worsened by my team's play. It was like they'd suddenly forgotten how to play baseball.

I huddled up our troops and *demanded* that they get busy and "go out and kick their [rears]." Except I didn't say "rears."

Well, that didn't help at all. It was out of my usual character, and my kids all looked at me like they had been hit with stun guns.

The coaches had a case of lockjaw. I was kind of wondering who had just yelled that stupid instruction, and we broke huddle, where we proceeded to get killed for the rest of the game.

So we go home that night, and my wife firmly asks me if I'm going to apologize to Will and the boys for what I said. (How did she know? Mothers always find out this stuff.)

"Yes," I said. "I was going to kind of mention it tomorrow."

"No," Suzanne said, "are you going to *apologize*?"

"Yeah, that's what I meant."

Ouch. Pride.

The next morning, game time. Before we did anything, I called the Mustangs over, including the dads, and pulled them close. "Guys, yesterday I said something really stupid and out of line. There is no excuse for the way I talked about what I wanted you guys to go do. I was frustrated, but that is still no excuse. When you cuss like that, it just shows you aren't smart enough or good enough to go out and take care of your business like a man. I let those guys get to me, so actually their strategy worked. I am sorry. Do you all forgive me?"

Man what a great bunch of kids. They had already started nodding before I asked. They knew what I was saying. They were so ready to get this over and let me know they forgave me. The dads were obviously in a kind of different situation, but they clearly were pleased with the admission and the example. They were awesome.

Oh, and we made it all the way to the finals in the tournament. That obnoxious team got eliminated before that.

Guilt is a horrible thing to live with. We all sin. We all have made mistakes. We can all be forgiven. Grace is a wonderful thing.

Don't be afraid to ask.

Don't be afraid to receive.

You'll feel a lot better.

CHAPTER 13

THE BLUE'S-EYE VIEW

"(I TELL PARENTS OF MY 13 AND 14 YEAR-OLD UMPIRES THAT) UMPIRING IS A WONDERFUL LIFE EXPERIENCE. IT TEACHES YOUNG PEOPLE TO BE CONFIDENT IN THEMSELVES, TO LEARN HOW TO MAKE QUICK, TOUGH DECISIONS IN DIFFICULT SITUATIONS; TO STAND UP TO THAT DECISION AND NOT BACK DOWN. IT TEACHES THEM HOW TO REACT IN HEATED MOMENTS, HOW TO DEAL WITH PEOPLE IN HEATED MOMENTS. IT TEACHES THEM TO ACT LIKE AN 'ADULT' WHEN THAT 'ADULT' IS ACTING LIKE A JUVENILE. THESE ARE ALL LIFE TRAINING TECHNIQUES THAT THEY CAN USE THROUGHOUT THEIR ADULT LIVES."

MIKE ETNIRE

CHAPTER 13: THE BLUE'S-EYE VIEW

I said earlier on that I've experienced this great game of baseball from every possible angle. I was a player. I was a coach. I was a parent.

But there was one crucial part of the game that I had never done:

Umpire.

As this project rolled along, I realized that, if I really wanted it to be comprehensive, I needed to put on the gear. I needed to become "Blue." (Umpires wear a blue uniform, and the nickname stuck.)

So I did it. I put on the mask for a summer. This is what I learned.

• • • • • •

The first thing I noticed was the nervousness. As a player, I usually started a game nervous, but after I got my first hit or scored a run or nabbed that vicious line drive in the gap, the nervousness would go away.

As a coach, my team, whether they played well and won or went off the cliff and lost, there was always a time during the game when the outcome was finally decided, and the nervousness would go away.

As a parent, whether my kids were having a great game or a terrible game, they would always do something to make me proud, and the nervousness would go way.

As an umpire, the nervousness *never went away*.

From the moment I walked onto the field until the moment the last out was called, I was nervous. Just a nervous tension the whole time. I enjoyed the experience, but was always aware that something could go wrong at any minute, and it all would depend on me making the right call.

For the first time in my entire baseball career, I had control over everything that happened on that field. Both teams, all parents, the strike zone, the speed of the game...I could do whatever I wanted. I had the ultimate authority. I found I didn't enjoy that feeling very much, and here's why. I knew I could get blamed for *everything* that went wrong.

But I was still a Keeper. Umpires are Keepers, too.

"Blue" is not generally a term of affection. It's just how parents, coaches, and players got my attention.

"Hey, Blue!"

"Blue, what was the call?"

"Time out, Blue."

"What's the count, Blue?"

"Good job, Blue."

"You stink, Blue!"

"Terrible call, Blue!"

"Great call, Blue!"

"Come on, Blue—that pitch was outside!"

"Come on, Blue—that pitch was inside!"

"Come on, Blue—that pitch was high!"

"Come on, Blue—that pitch was low!"

"Come on, Blue—he was safe by a mile!"

"Come on, Blue—he was out by five feet!"

"Come on, Blue—are we watching the same game?"

"Come on, Blue—call the fourth grade strike zone!"

(This was my favorite. I didn't know there was a strike zone specific to fourth grade.)

Blue has always been my favorite color, so I kind of liked being called "Blue."

Until now, I'd always been called "Coach," so every time someone yelled "Coach!" I turned my head. Took me awhile to realize I was no longer Coach; I was Blue.

But I was also still a Keeper.

I was still close to the kids, and I loved being called "Blue," because it meant I could still talk to them. When I went onto the field, I would talk to the kids, but I also looked into the stands at the faces of the parents, this time with a Blue's-eye view. Their faces were full of anxiety, hope, worry, excitement, fear, happiness, smiles, frustration.

I got to hand the eight-year-old catcher his mask every

time it came off. And every time he would thank me.

I got to stand in hundred-degree heat, trying to cover three bases at once, with throws going all over the place, and get called "lazy" and "overpaid" by parents who disagreed with me. There was the time I wondered who set the bases at a distance that *every stinking play* was a bang-bang play so that I was wrong in the eyes of 50% of the crowd.

For the first time in my career, I felt like an evil presence and that my only purpose was to be the lightning rod of blame when things went south.

• • • • • •

I think every coach should be Blue for at least two games a year. Just two. That's all you'd need to convince you to appreciate Blue. Being a little league umpire is very difficult. It's just not fair when coaches and parents add to the heat on every call.

One year, while I was playing triple-A ball in the Pacific Coast League, I struck out 27 times in 520 at-bats. That is not many strikeouts, and I tell you that to let you know that *I know* the strike zone. But when a ten-year-old kid throws a 31 mph fastball with a 38 mph crosswind, I can tell you that it <u>looks</u> like a strike at least three times before it ever hits the catcher's mitt. I was amazed! I've had 20/15 vision my whole life, but calling balls and strikes in the little league was such a challenge it made me question my eyesight.

Just two games. That should calm everyone down.

If fans knew what Blue hears, and how it could affect their team, I think they'd change what they say. We're humans, too. And most of the guys you call Blue in little league—and even high school or college—are just guys who love the game and are trying to still be around it, while making a little bit of money. As Blue, I realized my imperfections and just how difficult the job was. I didn't need anyone in the stands aggravating that for me.

Parents, after your coach does his two games as Blue, ask him about it. Ask him how it feels to be yelled at, screamed at, and blamed.

The most nervous I've ever been in my life was when I had to call a state game or a national tournament game. It was like I was sitting on a powder keg just waiting to explode. From the serenity of the 8:00 a.m. start on a beautiful Saturday morning to the chaos that would eventually break out with a close play at the plate, it was all just one big tense threat.

Things are getting out of control. News reports of irate parents and coaches attacking an umpire because they didn't like a call are all too frequent. People are getting hurt and beaten. People are going to jail.

Here's something to think about: third-degree assault happens when a person inflicts substantial bodily harm on another person or assaults a minor. Carries up to five years in prison and a fine of $10,000.

Second-degree assault is the same thing, but with a dangerous weapon (and a baseball bat is considered a dangerous weapon), you're looking at up to seven years in prison and a fine of $14,000.

If that doesn't get your attention, nothing will.

Keeper, if you feel that anger coming up, just get away. Like Jeff Easterday, my first coaching buddy, used to say, "Just take a walk." Seriously, just take a walk.

Your team will be fine. Go home. Don't go from the dugout to a prison cell. Just don't. Get out of there with your anger and misplaced frustration. Go talk to someone who knows how to listen.

• • • • • •

I say this stuff for the 10% of Keepers out there who are having a hard time being Keepers. I'd say about 90% of you are doing a great job.

Keepers love to be able to stand in the gap and protect their kids.

Keepers love to be able to protect other people's kids.

Keepers put it on the line.

Keepers see the big picture.

Keepers are not afraid of challenges.

Keepers are not afraid of helping kids along the way.

Keepers realize mothers are *very* serious about their babies. And that mothers are not afraid of Keepers, even if they're name is "Blue." Just smile at their babies and be nice to them.

· · · · · ·

I saw a lot of good things as a Keeper in Blue. I saw welcoming dugouts, where each child was welcomed after great plays, bad plays, long innings, final outs, rough times.

I saw grace under pressure. I saw coaches who held their tongue and checked their tempers, especially while their kids were on the field.

I saw teams who knew how to play the game, but didn't boast about it.

I saw coaches who didn't yell on every single play.

I saw coaches who hardly coached and just let the kids have fun.

I saw teams that had been so well coached they knew exactly what to do at all times, free to play.

I saw fun and laughter and hugs and encouragement coming from the players themselves.

I saw excitement and cheering. The good kind of yelling.

I saw great sportsmanship, respect, and continual caring to explain puzzling situations.

I saw a love of the game. Keepers all moving as one to help these kids down the road of life while teaching them the tools of the Sandlot.

But in the midst of all this good, I saw a lot of bad, too.

I saw the bad kind of yelling. The worst thing of all.

I saw kids full of fear in the dugouts, worried they would get hammered for their mistakes.

I saw coaches who met their players *before* they got to the dugout so they could hammer them for their mistakes ... anything but a welcoming dugout.

I saw kids wilting under pressure. Crying, even on teams that gave the appearance of looking great, but that cracked under the pressure and heat.

I saw screaming, on every pitch, just for the sake of screaming *something*.

I saw ten-year-old kids with blank looks on their faces, wondering why they were getting yelled at so loudly.

I saw coaches yell at everyone but themselves for blunders they'd committed.

I saw kids who didn't know what they were doing, and the frustration that came from that.

I saw friends looking for cover from the heat—literally and figuratively.

I saw a lot as Blue.

· · · · · ·

After a summer of watching, it dawned on me that, as the ultimate authority of the game, I had the ultimate responsibility for the way it would—and should—be played. I realized the way I entered the field would set the tone for the way the game would go. I learned I had responsibilities, too. I learned ...

That a simple smile goes a long way with a parent. It certainly doesn't hurt.

That I needed to have a strike zone that was as consistent as possible.

That I needed to be a hustler who worked hard to cover all the bases.

That I had to have a kind spirit toward the kids.

That I was an honest person honestly trying to do a great job.

That I would blow calls, and needed to admit it and get help from another Blue to make a correction.

That I had to have a non-confrontational attitude.

That I owed coaches and parents a simple explanation now and then, just to make sure a rule was correct.

That, as Blue, I could turn this place into a *Sandlot*.
Just like it should be.
Play ball.

CHAPTER 14

THE RIDE HOME

"WE WEREN'T ALWAYS THE BEST TEAM OUT THERE, NOR DID WE HAVE THE BEST LINE-UP FROM TOP TO BOTTOM. WE DID HOWEVER, HAVE THE MOST FUN. FOR THOSE REASONS, WE ALL LOVED THE GAME TREMENDOUSLY."

WYLIE
PRAIRE PANTHER '97-'98
MIAMI OF OHIO GRADUATE SCHOOL

CHAPTER FOURTEEN: THE RIDE HOME

In writing this book, my goal was to encourage parents and coaches and teachers to enjoy their kids on their journey through little league. I was a pretty good athlete. I have the mindset of an athlete, I love to compete. I am so thankful that I played the game with my kids the way I did. I have not always been perfect, but by the grace of God, I have been able to *be* there. My goal for you whether you are a parent, coach, teacher, friend or whoever is that you have no regrets with the effort you put forth. While I made some mistakes along the line, I have no regrets.

At the very end of my time writing this book, I had an incredibly special coffee that lasted over two hours with a dear friend, Coach Dick Kramer. Coach Kramer was Matthew's coach in high school, and is now the Principal of a large high school in Kansas City. Like my other great friends in this book, his input and influence on my life and on Matthew's has been significant.

The wisdom of Coach Kramer's words were an absolute stamp on what I was trying to accomplish. As a coach, educator, administrator, parent, friend, and coach of my kid, he wrapped it all up. As insightful and helpful as everyone has been to me on this project, I dare say this is as critical and encouraging to a parent as any. *Any* parent or coach can do this and understand it:

"From *day one*, when they come right out of the womb, talk to your child. You want your child to talk to you, so you need to talk to your child. Great parenting isn't going to guarantee your kid will make only great decisions; great parenting is being there when they make a bad one. Let them know you are glad they told you, and don't be so quick to judge. Be their anchor and support system so they can let you help them."

As my buddy Lee says, "Tell them to always run to you, not from you, no matter what!"

Coach Kramer closed with this simple phrase that all of us Keepers should take to heart: "Every message you send is received."

What message are you sending?

The ride home, after the game, is one of the most critical and influential times for a Keeper.

This is what happens on the ride home, through the eyes of my boys and some of the kids I coached...

My son Drew said, "As a child, my baseball dreams developed a great deal in the passenger seat of my dad's car. With Royals' talk radio on the airwaves in the background, Pops and I would talk about the lineup and who had been playing well for my little league team, the Panthers. Then we'd talk about where we were going to eat."

Will P., graduating this year from TCU - "Coach, I appreciate all the lessons you have taught me both about life and baseball. As a coach, you and [the other coaches] allowed us to succeed and fail, but insisted that we had fun while doing it. As to my rides home after the game, they were always the same. My father would say how great I played that day no matter how poor or little I played."

John - "The thing I loved about the rides home with my dad was we would talk about the game for a little while. Then I would get quiet and my dad would know I was through talking. He would reach over, turn on the radio and we would just head home."

Will S. - "I will never forget some of the conversations we've had coming home from 3& 2. I will miss those the most because I could never get tired of you telling me how good I am." Take that special time after your little league games and tell your child you love them. Never assume they know that.

My buddy Gary with the Cardinals made a wonderful statement about the Keeper's role at this time: "On the ride home, the game is over. The reason for the trip was to play the game. Now the game is over. In a kid's mind, he got excited about it, looked forward to it and he is on to the next thing."

Don't make the mistake of being a critic on the ride home, stewing over a loss or making too much of a victory. This is the time to let your kid know how great they are, regardless of the way they played. That they're valuable to you, and that you're glad they're your kid. It's a time of encouragement. A time to soak in your kid's *kid*-ness.

I've said it all throughout this book, Keepers: the time goes by too, too quickly to make it anything but fun. Your kids will figure out life along the way. They'll figure out the fundamentals of the game.

And one day, you'll drop that kid off somewhere—college, most likely—and then you'll ride home by yourself. And you'll miss those rides home, and you'll either wish you'd made the most of them, or you'll be thankful that you used that time wisely.

Every message you send is received.

Make the ride home the best part of the game.

You can do it, Keeper.

You can do anything you want, as long as it's fun.

You're in the Sandlot.

KEEPERSOFTHESANDLOT.COM
Coaching, Parenting and Playing for Keeps

By Bill Severns

To Order additional copies of
KEEPERS OF THE SANDLOT
contact us at
www.keepersofthesandlot.com

For information on personal consultations,
parent clinics and speaking engagements
contact us at
www.keeprsofthesandlot.com
Follow us during the baseball season on our blog,
www.sandlotkeeper.blogspot.com.
And remember, have fun!,
play fearlessly!
and have a great season!!

Keepers of the Sandlot
ISBN 978-0-615-27726-4
Copyright © 2009 by Bill Severns

About the Author

Gene Stephenson, one of the winningest coaches in college baseball history, says that "Bill Severns worked harder than any player that I ever had... because he needed to." As a sophomore at his Tulsa (Hale) high school, Severns was cut from the baseball team on the first day of practice. Seven years later, he finished a college baseball career at the University of Oklahoma as the Sooners career leader in games played, hits, extra base hits, total bases, triples, stolen bases, and runs scored.

Severns hard work paid off in college. A starter from day one, he played on conference championship teams and in the College World Series four consecutive years. His teams compiled a record of 178-47, a .791 winning percentage. Despite being drafted by the New York Yankees, the fabled franchise of his boyhood hero – fellow Oklahoman Mickey Mantle (both wore number 7) – in the June 1974 draft, then by the San Francisco Giants in January 1975, Severns returned to Norman for his senior year. After serving as team co-captain and president of the OU Fellowship of Christian Athletes while completing his Bachelors degree in Business Administration, Severns became first round draft choice of the Milwaukee Brewers in the June 1975 secondary draft.

Severns played professionally for six years in the Brewers organization, batting .300 for Vancouver at the Triple-A level, before retiring from baseball to raise a family with his wife Suzanne.

Severns involvement in the game since then harkens back to the final weeks of his college career. In May 1975, quoted by a newspaper columnist, he said, "Coaching is a learning process, too, I guess." It was a good guess. Now, with twenty-three years of experience as a youth baseball coach, he has learned a lot in the process. *Keepers of the Sandlot* is his first book, answering the call to share a lifetime of experience with others.

Bill and Suzanne have been married for 38 years and live in Prairie Village, Kansas. They have four children, Matthew, Sarah, Drew and Will. They are proud grandparents of 8, David, Annie, Ruthie, Naomi, Sullivan, Lillian, Jake and Claudia.